the Electric Woman

OTHER BOOKS BY MARABEL MORGAN

The Total Woman
Total Joy
The Total Woman Cookbook—Handbook for Kitchen Survival

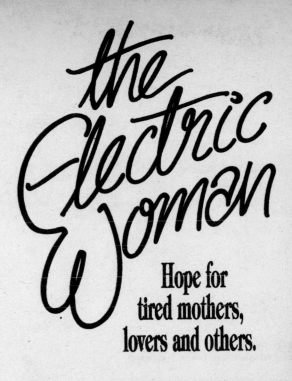

the Electric Woman

Hope for
tired mothers,
lovers and others.

Marabel Morgan

KEY-WORD BOOKS
AN IMPRINT
OF
WORD BOOKS, PUBLISHER
WACO, TEXAS
A DIVISION OF
WORD INCORPORATED

THIS BOOK IS DEDICATED

To every woman who gained five pounds,
    Or broke her nail,
    Or dropped a plate,
    Or changed a diaper,
    Or lost her glasses,
    Or got a runner,
    Or burned the roast,
    Or waited to check out,
    Or argued with the repairman,
        . . . this week.
For all others, this book is unnecessary reading.
    Please write your own—
        and rush me your first copy.

CONTENTS

WITH SINCERE APPRECIATION

Thank you, Charlie—
>   For your help in writing this book,
>>   For your prayers during my downers,
>>>   For your praise during my uppers,
>>>>   And for your love through it all.

Thank you, dear Laura and Michelle—
>   For lighting up my life in living color.

Thank you, Friends—
>   For your stories which unfold on these pages.
>>   Your lives have been an inspiration to me.

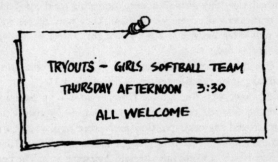

TRYOUTS - GIRLS SOFTBALL TEAM
THURSDAY AFTERNOON   3:30
ALL WELCOME

The coach had just tacked up the poster on the bulletin board and already a small group of ninth-grade girls had gathered around. "Should we try out, Michelle?" asked Rachel hesitantly.

"Why not? Let's go for it," she said. "Let's all try out," she urged the rest of the jean-clad onlookers.

That night sitting around the dinner table, Michelle, the youngest member of the Morgan household, told us about her decision.

Her twelfth-grade sister, Laura, said, "I think it's great, Mitch."

"So do I," agreed her father, Charlie.

"Well, that makes it unanimous," I added. Although Michelle wasn't exactly major league softball material, the competition and exercise would be good for her.

The next morning Michelle was up at six o'clock. Wonder of wonders. As I dropped her off at school, she slammed the car door and yelled back to me, "Don't forget, Mom. Practice isn't over until 5:00 tonight."

Later that afternoon, when I drove up to watch the last few minutes of practice, Michelle was standing in center field with all the other girls who were competing for the position of outfielder—all seventeen of them. They were almost wall to wall. *There couldn't be a hit,* I thought. *There's no place for the ball to drop.*

Just then I heard the coach yell, "OK Sam, come on in and take some practice swings. Then that's it."

A tremor went through the players. Sam was up. Sam was a legend. She was the captain of the team, the shortstop, the pitcher, and any other position she wanted to play. She was a combination of Pete Rose, Reggie Jackson, and Babe Ruth.

Sam was in a world unto herself. Awesome Sam. The best thing about Sam was that she was on our side.

Sam stepped up to bat. Outfielders started running backward expecting home-run balls in the next county. Mothers on the bleachers whispered to each other, "Sam's at bat!" I jumped out of the car to get a better view.

Sam slammed the first pitch into center field like a rocket, fortunately missing everyone.

That could kill somebody, I thought. I was concerned for Michelle's safety, as ball after ball bounced off the roof of the science building.

"One more, Sam," yelled the coach. The pitcher lobbed the ball toward the plate and then headed for cover. Sam pulled it into left field toward Michelle. "Oh no," I groaned. "I just hope she gets out of the way!"

I saw arms and legs flailing as she headed for the screaming bullet. Michelle's arms shot up in the air and she trapped the ball in her borrowed mitt. She held on as she fell backward.

"You caught it, Michelle! You caught it! That's my girl!" I screamed from the sideline, jumping up and down as if the New York Yankees had just won the World Series.

All eyes turned toward me. Michelle's withering look from left field brought me back to earth.

Practice was over. I felt embarrassed, but not half as much as Michelle.

Catcher in the Wry

The next Thursday afternoon, just a day before the big game with the Vikings, Michelle made the team. I'll spare you the trauma of the final cuts.

On the way home, I told her, "I'm really proud of you, honey. How did you do?"

She paused and said, "Well, Mistake Number One— Never tell the coach you don't care where you play. Our catcher broke her leg today, and the coach asked who wanted to play catcher. Everybody said no but me, so now I'm it."

Her lower lip quivered as she whispered, "Mom, I can't even throw, let alone catch! But the worst thing," she moaned, "is the game tomorrow with the Vikings. I'm so-o-o scared."

When Charlie came home that evening, I announced cheerfully, "Meet the new catcher of the Spartan softball team!"

"Yeah," Michelle sighed, as she looked up from her homework, "and I don't even know what a catcher is supposed to do."

Charlie spent the evening playing catch with her in the living room. He used rolled-up socks instead of balls. Michelle practiced crouching, and I was the batter with a broomstick. It was a cram course on catching. I wish someone had videotaped it.

The next day was the big game at the Vikings' field across town. I couldn't attend because of previous plans, but I could hardly wait to meet the team when they returned.

At 6:25 P.M. the old yellow bus rumbled to a stop. Two dozen grimy, teenage faces searched for family cars parked on the grass. It was immediately evident from their forlorn expressions who had won the game.

When she was seated in the car, Michelle proclaimed, "Well, today I learned Mistake Number Two. Never wait until the day of the game to try on the whole catcher's outfit."

She gave a blow-by-blow explanation all the way home. At game time, the coach had helped Michelle put on the catcher's gear. First, the shin pads from ankle to knees, then the bulky chest-protector, then the heavy face-mask, and finally the over-sized glove.

She could hardly walk. In fact, it wasn't until the second inning that she realized she could bend her knees. Crouched straight-legged "like a toy soldier," she bent over at the waist in a very vulnerable position.

"Once when Hildy threw the ball to me," she recounted, "it was over my head. I tried to jump left, but I couldn't bend my knees. I fell on my back and couldn't get up. The umpire had to pull me up. I was mortified, Mom. He showed me that I could bend my knees."

"What was the score?" I asked, but then wished I hadn't.

Michelle gave me that look reserved by teenagers who doubt their parents were born in the same century.

"Are you kidding?" she said cynically. "We got killed, 29–3."

"Well, did you get any hits?"

"Nope. Was only up once, but I got to know their entire team. In fact, I learned most of them by their first names since they were up to bat so much."

"Well, if you played the whole game," I asked, "how come you were only up to bat one time?"

"They called the game after three innings. I think they called it a 'mercy killing'!"

Soggy Saga

Such is the adventure of a ninth-grade catcher. How could life be more bleak?

But I knew exactly how she felt, and I have recalled her experience on more than one occasion in the months since then. There have been many days when I too have wished for a mercy killing.

Like last Monday. It started out as a muggy summer day. I had high hopes of writing in order to meet a deadline. Charlie left for work early and I hurried to my desk before the girls woke up. I had been waiting for this day for weeks.

I picked up the pen and the doorbell rang, simultaneously. Murphy's Law couldn't have planned it better.

Who could it be this early in the morning? A water-meter reader stood holding his clipboard and scratching his head. "Ma'am, you got water running somewhere?"

"No, I don't."

"Well, your meter's going crazy. It's registering a gallon a minute, so there's a leak somewhere. I'll keep looking, but if I don't find anything, don't worry. I'll report it when I get back tonight."

"Be cool," I told myself, as I closed the door. "It's only water. So what? They won't charge us if it's their fault. Forget the water meter."

The doorbell had awakened Michelle, who stumbled out chattering over a nightmare (something about our house being on fire). She then busied herself making cinnamon muffins, and I escaped back to the bedroom.

The phone rang. It was Charlie. "Chuck Hall's coming for dinner tonight," he said. "Nothing fancy. Just put on an extra plate. I'll bring home chicken if you want."

"No, it's OK. And when you get home, maybe you can find our leak." I hung up before he could ask any questions.

As I picked up the pen again, Michelle came rushing into the room.

"Mom," she whimpered in an anguished tone. "It's Bill! He's stuck."

Bill? Who's Bill? Then I remembered. Bill was Michelle's new kitten.

I followed Michelle to Bill's new quarters—our garage— mentally fortifying myself for the worst. Bill the Cat had wedged himself under a stack of chairs and was meowing at the top of his tiny lungs.

"Michelle, lift the chairs off one by one and get him out. He's not hurt, he's just scared."

Hopeful that this project would keep her occupied, I retreated quickly inside. But when I returned to the bedroom, I felt water slosh on my bare feet.

"What in the world?" I said out loud. The carpet was soaking wet! The water-meter man *was* right! But where was the water coming from?

As I turned to search, the phone rang again. I started to slosh back through the surf to the phone, but Laura had already answered it.

"Mom!" she squealed. "The basketball team from college is coming in tonight from Bolivia. I told Dave to have them all stop by for dessert."

I shivered in the wet carpet. What to do first? The water was rising. High tide soon. Dessert would have to wait.

Then a light dawned. The plumber had fixed the toilet last week. I headed for the bathroom. That was it! A steady stream of water running from the pipes was flooding the floor and apparently seeping through the tiles of the bathroom into the bedroom.

Laura interrupted my feet-soaking reverie, "But it's no big deal, Mom. There are only fifteen basketball players and two coaches."

Oh. Only fifteen huge, hungry ballplayers, that's all. Nothing to it. Just roll, baby, roll.

I looked at the clock in the kitchen. It was 9:48 A.M. The day was barely under way, but I was ready to call the Funny Farm for a pickup.

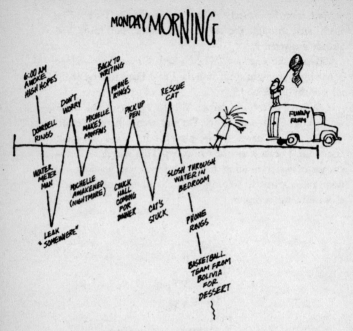

Former baseball pitcher Larry "Satchel" Paige once said, "Don't look back, man. Something might be gaining on you!"

Gaining on me? Are you kidding? Looking back over my shoulder on that Monday morning, I could see a semi with a load of bricks bearing down on me, bouncing off my bumper!

In a short span of time on that particular Monday, my nervous system was bombarded with all sorts of interruptions, each one hitting me like an electrical shock. These negative impulses came from all directions without any warning—some biggies and lots of lesser ones—and I was left reeling from their jolts. I felt like Ms. Lightning Rod. An electric woman, with a blown fuse!

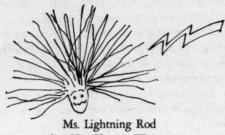

Ms. Lightning Rod
(alias The Electric Woman)

A week has passed since that infamous Monday, and although it seemed chaotic, it really wasn't. It was just another Monday.

Those interruptions are called Life. None of them were tragic or life-changing, but they were unsettling nonetheless. We fixed the leak. The rug dried. I met the deadline. The basketball team didn't show up, and Bill the Cat survived The Great Chair Scare. Once again I realized that life is what happens when we are sitting around making other plans.

All of us have our downers all day long, every day. Some days they're worse than others. Your same Monday may have been far worse than mine. But the essence of life is accepting the bad with the good, the downers with the uppers. Since we can't run away, we must face these negative charges and improvise moment by moment. Life is the art of improvisation.

Ben Franklin had the right idea. During a driving thunderstorm while everyone else was huddled inside playing Early American Trivia by candlelight, ol' Ben was outside flying a kite, trying to *attract* lightning. And though he knew its dangers, he had a hunch that electricity had a powerful constructive potential—a potential to light our homes, cook our food, and change our environment, and he was trying to harness it. The negative impulses that bombard us emotionally all day long also have that same constructive potential.

The first question then is: How can we redirect these electrical impulses and cause them to work *for* us rather than *against* us?

And the second is: How can we create an environment so that uppers are more likely to happen than downers?

Is it possible to channel all this electricity, these exasperating lightning bolts, into a rainbow?

You bet it is! In fact, that's exactly the plan.

It is possible to convert these electrical impulses—the downers of everyday life—into a life fully charged with power and light. The result? Not a woman with a blown fuse, but an electric woman who transforms the high voltage of life's downers into positive energy.

In the pages ahead, I will discuss how to cope with downers, and how to hope for uppers, and if we make it that far, how to share it with others.

Would you like to join me? All ready? Let's go. Let's follow the rainbow as we cross the first bridge, "How to Cope with Downers."

1

Coping
with Downers

Four Ways to Make It through the Plight

1. Customize

2. Cleanse

3. Challenge

4. Claim

Four Ways to Make It through the Plight

'Twas the night before Christmas, and I was jogging to run off some extra holiday calories. A young friend of mine from San Francisco who was visiting his grandparents (our neighbors) rode up on his bike.

As I continued to jog, he rode alongside bringing me up to date on the news of his family. Then he asked if I had been writing. "It so happens that I am working on a new manuscript," I puffed.

"What's it about?" he asked.

For me it's hard enough to jog, let alone jog and talk at the same time. "It's about coping with downers," I gasped, and before he could ask a follow-up question, I took the initiative, and asked, "But you probably don't have any downers in high school, do you, John?"

"Oh, I sure do," he answered. "The biggest downer in my life was this month when one of my girlfriends was stabbed to death."

"What?" I asked, suddenly stopping in my tracks.

"And the second biggest downer," he continued, "came when another girlfried of mine was charged with killing her. She was arrested for murder last week and goes to trial in February!"

So much for my idle notion that teenage troubles are pocket-sized problems. Downers are no respecter of persons or age, and unfortunately, no one is immune even if he has already been zapped once. Sometimes lightning does strike twice, or more.

All day long you and I struggle with downers. They may be as minor as a broken nail or as serious as the death of a loved one. These negative impulses cause internal turmoil and stress. Stress is said to be the Number One disease of the '80s. It takes its toll on all of us. When the circuits of our nervous system become overloaded, serious health problems can result—ulcers, kidney problems, and strokes, to name a few.

Drs. Thomas H. Holmes and Richard H. Rahe have developed a test to determine the degree of intensity of stress under various circumstances. This simple exercise, published recently in a *Time* magazine advertorial, is helpful to all of us who run on the Twentieth Century Fast Track.

How deep is your downer? To rate yourself, check the events from the following list that affected you this past year, and then add up the total.

HOW DEEP IS YOUR DOWNER?

Event	Stress Points
Death of a spouse	100
Divorce	73
Jailing or institutionalization	63
Death of a close family member	63
Major injury or illness	53
Marriage	50
Fired from job	47
Pregnancy	40
Birth of a baby	39
Changing to different line of work	36
Mortgage or loan for major purchase	31
Foreclosure	30
Departure of child from home	29
Trouble with in-laws	29
Outstanding personal achievement	28
Wife starting or stopping job	26
Change in residence	20
New school	20
Major change in sleeping habits	16
Major change in eating habits	15
Vacation	13
Christmas	12
Minor legal violations (traffic tickets, etc.)	11

If your total is 300 or more, you may be a candidate for a heart attack. In fact, any stress score over 150 may still be in a danger zone. So, to be on the safe side, doctors recommend that you reevaluate your life and try to reduce the stress factors.

The stress test deals mainly with the A-number-1, heavy duty, solid-state, all-purpose, wipe-out downers, but does not measure the lesser stress-inducers like losing the car keys. It fails to measure any distractions less major than a traffic ticket.

I can think of loads of trauma-inducing activities which a home executive encounters all day long. So can any card-carrying member of the White Diapers and Potty Manners Detail! The daily list is endless . . . and constant.

Feed baby.

Feed Fred.

Wash baby.

Cook dinner.

Change baby.

Feed baby.

And so on.

Although none of these may cause a computer short out, when they hit (sometimes in waves), they are major. The cumulative effect of a baby's constant cries, for example, is probably more stressful to a mother than 31 points for taking out a loan to buy a refrigerator!

Other mini stress-inducers that we all face are simply part of a day's work. Occupational hazards. They go with the territory. Here are some examples that I face all the time. The stress points are my own designation.

DAILY MINI-DOWNERS

Event	Stress Points
Hear siren	5
Hear siren of police car	7
Hear siren of police car behind you	20

Event	Stress Points
Plate crashes on floor	8
Orange tastes sour	1/2
Fingernails scratch on blackboard	7
Pencil lead breaks	1
Pencil lead breaks, only one available	8
Long traffic light	2
Light changes, but car ahead stalls	8
Driver behind you leans on horn	12
Sit behind a cigar smoker	6
Surly cashier	3
Flat tire	7
Stub toe in night	10
Hot taco sauce (El Scorcho)	4
Break nail on way to party	11

Score yourself as follows:

1–10	Sheer Bliss
11–20	Shoot the Rapids
21–30	Edge of Panic

Big Brother

Your internal stress levels now can be measured by all sorts of unique methods and devices. Here are a few:

• *Body Language.* Your body indicates stress by revealing telltale, abnormal signals. Myriads of books on body language give tip-offs to look for—the folded arms, the pressed lips, the constant shuffling, the heavy breathing, and so on.

• *Lie Detectors.* Stress levels can be measured electronically through the use of a polygraph or lie detector. The polygraph operates on the premise that a lie will cause guilt, and guilt will cause stress, and stress will produce behavior or body signals that are measurable. In most cases, you can't keep your system from revealing what you feel inside.

Now, a mini-polygraph is on the market. This gadget, called a voice-stress analyzer, approximately the size of a hand-held calculator, can tell by voice signals if you're lying, and worst of all—you may not even be aware that it's being used.

I mentioned this to a friend who has been dating a suspicious character for two months, and she wanted to know where she could rent one "for about a week."

I doubt if the Spot-A-Lie can be rented, and even if it could, the waiting list would be a mile long!

Imagine what happens if the American Civil Liberties Union gets involved. When your husband comes home, you will first need to advise him of his rights, "Honey, before I ask you about your sales meeting, I must advise you that your voice vibrations may be used against you. You have the right to remain silent.

"Now, about 'Ugly Susan,' your new assistant. Want to run her description by me one more time?"

• *Wiggle Seat.* Another type of stress/lie detector is called a wiggle seat. Instead of measuring voice stress, it measures muscle contractions where you sit.

Really. An electric chair!

Talk about Big Brother! Not only must you be careful what you say, but where you sit, and how you wiggle!

Well, if all this newfangled, high-tech, snoop-and-sleuth stuff keeps up, who knows? Someday soon we may be able to press a button at the end of the day and get a print-out, or perhaps play a video game with our day's emotions.

When Fred comes home from the office, instead of asking, "How was your day, Hon?" you can just plug him in and press his button.

But more important than all these gadgets is understanding how downers impact the nervous system.

Let's try a little experiment for a moment. First find a pad and pencil. Do it. It's worth the effort.

Draw a line across the page from left to right. Now, chart your morning's activities as either uppers or downers. Do this chronologically.

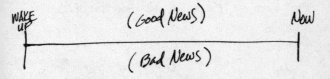

You may think, "Well, nothing momentous has happened between the time I woke up and now. I just got up and went to work (or took Johnny to school)."

More than likely nothing momentous has happened, but it's that bundle of mini-uppers and downers that I'm talking about—the water-meter reader, the phone interruptions, the college basketball team, the wet rug.

Think back on your day so far. I'll bet you could fill a few pages, right? Remember the realization when consciousness first surfaced? It was morning—time to face the world. Your back hurt or your blusher broke or your pantyhose got a run. All those little diddly-squat irritations took their toll on your raw nervous system early in the morning.

But then there was a bright side, too. Perhaps you saw glorious colors spilling across the eastern sky. Or maybe you heard a bird singing. Or you remembered, "Hey, I'm alive! I've got another day; let's get this show on the road."

Now take a look at your chart and see what you have. The chart shows just one brief period of your uppers and downers. But your brain has been keeping a record of all impulses since your birth—all day long and during sleep as well. With all these accumulated impulses over a lifetime, no wonder you feel pressure!

You and I each have a past. Yours may have been sordid or glorious or mundane. But now you stand where the "Past" meets the "Present" on the Time Line of Life.

Up to this point your "Past Graph" is full and finished. Your memory bank is filled with ups and downs. And there's absolutely nothing you can add to it or take from it. It's over.

Your future, however, is blank. Unknown, unwritten, and untrod. It will be what you will make of it.

Isn't that exciting? From this moment on, *you will be making history!*

Singer Wayne Cochrane concludes his concerts with these words, "Your dreams are what you were meant to be. What you become is what you settle for."

Don't settle for less than the best!

Now consider this. Before you go to bed tonight, you will probably have some downers.

Unfortunately this is true. And, according to Ginsberg's Theorem,

> "You can't win.
>> You can't break even.
>>> You can't even quit the game."

How depressing. (But don't give up. There are some surprises up ahead!)

Have you made your plans yet for today? Take a moment right now and list everything you need to do.

If your list looks anything like most of my friends', it's probably chock-full with carpooling, meetings, work, time with the kids, shopping, and so on.

But did you remember to leave any room for distractions? Or unexpected problems? If you haven't planned on any negatives, you'd better. It may rain on your parade. You may get a headache during the meeting. Or lose your keys. Or maybe just break a nail.

Joe Frazier, the former heavyweight boxing champion, reflecting back on his career once said, "One thing I learned is, life don't run away from people. Life runs *at* people."

That's true. You may be on top of the world, but then wake up one morning and find that the world has rolled over on you. Life throws you a curve and knocks you off schedule.

Excuse me, the spaghetti just boiled over on the stove. Unscheduled clean-up. I'll be right back.

Voltage Regulator

By tomorrow, can we be assured of some uppers? Not necessarily. For starters, I don't know for sure if I'll even be around tomorrow. I don't know what's up ahead. I'm not assured of anything above the line. If I ever think, "I've got it made," I'm in big trouble.

On the other hand, if uppers should come, of course, I'll welcome them with open arms. You and I will have no problem in dealing with the uppers, right? We can handle success and fun times and parties.

Isn't that true? Most women I know seem well-equipped for fame, fortune, or beauty, if it should come their way.

We know we can handle the uppers, but how can we learn to deal with the downers that do us in? How can we make it through the plight?

In the next four chapters you'll find four ways for coping with downers. You can customize, cleanse, challenge, claim. It's a game plan that calls for meeting downers head-on *before* they hit. It works for me, and it can work for you, too.

CUSTOMIZE

After two weeks of school, six-year-old David came home one day crying.

"What's the matter, David?" his mother asked as he dropped his books on the floor. "Are you all right?"

"No," he moaned. "I'm just a big, fat zero. I can't do anything right. I'm nothing. Just a big, fat zero."

David is a first-grader in Boston, the son of a prominent dentist. He is not handicapped or underprivileged. He comes from a two-parent home. All of his necessities have been met, and that's what made his comments so surprising.

I have talked with many adults who have the same low self-esteem that David had. One woman from Tennessee asked, "Can you give some hope to a nobody?"

Feelings of inferiority are not always verbalized as they were in this woman's letter. Verbalized or not, if they exist, they have probably been there a long time. As Peanuts' cartoonist Charles Schultz said, "Losers get started early."

Why?

One reason may be that we live in a society that recognizes only the "beautiful people." Americans today, according to Randy Palmer, writing in the *Presbyterian Journal,* "are preoccupied with celebrity and drama, interested in form more than substance. We see Reggie Jackson or Cheryl Tiegs or Senator Kennedy or John Travolta on TV or magazine covers and we say to ourselves, 'He or she is somebody,' with the obvious, if unspoken, implication of that quote, 'I am nobody.' "

Our society puts a high premium on stardom, which explains the high sales of gossip newspapers at the checkout counter. If you are one of "the beautiful people," you are somebody. But if not, then you are nothing. In other words, you're either a hero or a zero. And most of us by society's definition are zeros.

Charlie is the lawyer for some of the Miami Dolphin football players, so when the Dolphins played the San Francisco 49ers in the Super Bowl, he traveled to California on the team plane. At the hotel, the players pushed their way through the lobby which was jammed with fans screaming for autographs. Cheers reverberated as the crowd recognized their favorite players.

Charlie was squeezed in between two huge linebackers when a young boy about nine years old noticed him. Surprised at seeing someone dressed in a suit, the boy asked Charlie, "Hey mister, are *you* somebody?"

So the question before the house is, "Are you somebody?" Whether you are an eighth-grade teacher or a newlywed or a mother of ten, are you somebody?

May I have the envelope, please?

The answer—"Absolutely!"

You are a unique person with untold potential. You were created for this time in history, for a very special purpose. You are not a creature of chance. You are a woman of destiny!

You were not made from an assembly line or stamped out with a cookie cutter. God made you unique. Think of it! There is no one else anywhere in the world exactly like you. Isn't that exciting? We don't have to do things like everyone else. We can customize our lives by capitalizing on our uniqueness and individuality.

In this chapter I want to share with you how to customize your self, your style, and your body.

CUSTOMIZE YOUR SELF

The picture on the Christmas card was irresistible to me, a colonial house nestled among sprawling oak trees. At the kitchen window, framed by ruffled curtains, a cranberry glass lamp beamed soft light across the new-fallen snow. The cozy scene called my name, inviting me to come on in.

As I gazed at the card, I nodded my head. That's what I long for, a picture perfect home. My dream home conjures up images of perfection, serenity, and living happily ever after, and it's always in the back of my mind.

Unfortunately, I have discovered that there will never be perfection on this earth, at least not in our household. Charlie and I will never have a perfect marriage because we're two imperfect people.

So, I have changed my attitude. Instead of something to be grasped, perfection has become a gentle goal for which to strive. After all these years I am learning to relax. Now I accept myself and others as imperfect, yet wonderful beings, distinct and different from one another.

When we were first married, Charlie was in tax law school at New York University. We lived in an apartment the size of a broom closet. But we turned it into a home— our home.

I will never forget that Sunday afternoon in late August when we drove into Greenwich Village. My heart pounded with anticipation as Charlie hauled boxes and I carried Laura over the threshold into our tiny apartment.

We had no furniture. Charlie piled his lawbooks and typewriter on a box in the corner while I investigated the kitchen that was big enough only for one body to stand in. At least there wouldn't be much to clean.

I was most concerned about the wood-splintering floor. How could my peachy-pink baby ever crawl on that awful floor?

The very next morning we headed for Macy's basement, and on a remnant pile, we found a beautiful piece of wool carpeting in the exact size that would fit our room.

I loved it. I patted it, felt its warmth, and admired the pattern of green and blue flowers scattered across the lavender blue background.

In my mind the carpet looked like a forest floor. I enhanced the illusion of living in a cool forest by using pots of ferns and philodendrons to fill in the corners. Each morning when I woke up and saw the rug, its beauty pulled a cord in my heart and I responded with joy.

Now it was time to do something to those four bare walls.

As we walked the streets of Greenwich Village each day, we passed many restaurants of all kinds, shapes, and smells.

In every direction there were whole new neighborhoods of shops and restaurants.

We decided to eat at a different place whenever we went out and take home a menu for the walls. Even restaurants we could not afford (which were most of them) consented to give us a menu. Pasted on our walls those menus looked terrific. Within a few months we had completely wallpapered the apartment.

Nothing fancy, but at least it was creative and cheap. We had taken a dumpy little apartment and customized it with our own touch.

Worth Reflecting

What I am within is revealed to others through my outward actions. My home, for instance, is an expression of what I am. Bam! There I am—my style and my self laid bare (almost) in the rooms of my house.

Is it any wonder that dirty, cluttered, ugly surroundings make a woman feel irritable and unraveled? How can you clear your mind and reach for the stars when you are knee-deep in debris?

As a woman thinks in her heart, so is she. When we lived in the Village, I learned that having my nest in order freed me to concentrate on more important issues—the inner person, for example.

I also discovered that customizing my nest worked hand in hand with customizing my self. As I experimented within my limited knowledge of decorating, I began to develop my style. I felt a sweet satisfaction and a strengthening of my own self-esteem.

If you want to feel better about yourself, a few environmental changes may help to lift your spirit. What's happening within your four walls? How can you add your special touch? Look around you. Do you need to clean it up or throw it out or do it over?

When we feel good about ourselves, we are better able to cope with life's problems. Dr. Robert Schuller, pastor of the Crystal Cathedral in Garden Grove, California, commissioned a Gallup Poll on self-esteem. In his book, *Self-Esteem: The New Reformation,* he revealed that people with a strong self-esteem:

—have a high moral and ethical sensitivity.
—have a high sense of family.
—view success in terms of relationships, not materialism.
—are more productive on the job.
—have a low incidence of chemical addiction.
—are likely to be involved in social and political activities.
—are generous with charitable and relief causes.

In short, people with a strong sense of self-esteem demonstrate qualities that benefit their environment, their country, and their family.

Trouble in Paradise

Remember the ancient story of Job? How relevant it still is today.

To put it in modern terms, Job was a wealthy rancher and tycoon. He ran City Hall. Mr. Clout. A member of the jet set. Mrs. Job wore designer jeans. Their kids drove imported chariots. They lived on the edge of the Mediterranean in a sprawling ranch house. Early "Dallas."

One day the Lord and Satan were discussing Job. They looked down on him while he watched the evening news with his feet propped up.

"Oh sure," said Satan, "no wonder he's so thankful. Look what he owns."

But the Lord told Satan that even if Job were to lose it all, he would not curse God.

Satan asked to test Job, and God let him do it. Satan zapped Job and took away everything he had—his cattle, sheep, servants, children, and even his health.

Talk about downers! Job went from the very top to the very bottom. From super upper to deadly downer. From the penthouse to the basement without an elevator!

With this tragedy of epic proportion, what was Job's greatest loss? What did he personally feel most grieved about?

His children? His cattle? His bank accounts? No. None of the above.

Judging from his writings, I believe that Job's greatest loss was the loss of respect, a direct threat to his self-esteem. And the terrible irony to Job was that he had done nothing wrong! He just got wiped out. Yet people mocked and laughed and scoffed at him. Such disrespect was almost too much to bear. Job wanted to die, but he remained faithful in his despair. He never cursed God.

(By the way, in case you've forgotten the rest of the story, it did have a happy ending. The Lord restored to Job everything he had lost, and more. In fact, twice as much. Back to the penthouse in a brand new highrise! But most important of all, Job found his own self to be intact; his character was vindicated.)

Perhaps you have been stripped of your dignity in some way. Maybe your downers have been catastrophic and you feel like giving up. But wait! Even if you're at the bottom of the pit, there is still hope. Your plans may have failed, but *you* haven't. *You* are still intact. You can rise from the ashes. You can begin anew. You. The resilient woman!

CUSTOMIZE YOUR STYLE

The sign in the country store read,

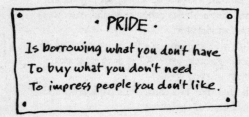

Why is it so important for us to impress other people? In this do-your-own-thing age, isn't it amazing how many crowd followers are still around?

At the next party you attend, do a little spot-check. Watch for the "in" designer outfits. Check the makes of cars in the driveway, the models of watches, and the hairstyles. These outward styles reflect the current fads, which change almost as often as the weather. When the fads change so does the crowd.

Why do we make ourselves miserable by trying to be like everybody else? Why do we care so much what others think? As the saying goes, "We wouldn't be so concerned about what people think of us, if we knew how seldom they do!"

Fearing that the crowd won't like the "real thing," we conform. We hide behind our masks. Howard Butt, in his book, *The Velvet Covered Brick,* says we play a game of "movable masks."

He explains, "In a religious group I shove up my religious mask: combination John Wesley, St. Francis and Father Divine. In a business group I use my business mask: John Hartford, Paul Getty, and Colonel Sanders. Most often I use my 'great-guy' mask: Arnold Palmer, Groucho Marx, and Mr. Clean. But these masks are bigger than anything I was built to carry. I've got hernias in my soul."

When we play the mask game, we lose touch with who we really are, and we become slaves to the crowd.

Dear Dead Duck

Our pastor, Steve Brown, told the story of a young boy who accidentally killed his grandmother's pet duck. He tried to bury it in the creek bed, but his sister Lucy had secretly witnessed the incident and let him know that she knew about it.

At dinner that night, she announced, "Grandma, Billy would like to do the dishes tonight."

Grandmother seemed surprised and asked, "Is that so, Billy?"

He kept his head down and muttered, "Yes, Grandma," while Lucy bit her lip to keep from laughing.

The next morning, as the children headed outside for their chores, Lucy said, "I think I'll go fishing this morning. Billy told me he wanted to do the chickens when he finished mowing. He just loves those chickens," she drolled, looking at a silent Billy. "*Don't* you, Billy?"

Billy never said a word, but shuffled toward the barn.

That afternoon on the porch, Lucy was sprawled on the swing while her grandmother rocked. When Billy trudged up covered with sweat and hay, Lucy said, "Oh hi, Billy. You're just in time."

"For what?" he growled.

"To start painting the chicken coop. We've still got a few hours left, and I told Grandma how excited you were about trying the new paint brush!"

In exasperation, Billy tore across the porch toward Lucy. His grandmother grabbed him. "Billy! Stop!"

Billy started to cry. Between sobs he confessed his wrong-doing of killing Grandmother's pet duck.

She replied softly, "I know all about it."

"You know?" Billy asked. "Then why didn't you say something?"

She answered gently, "I just wanted to see how long you'd be a slave to Lucy."

Seek the Chic

Are you a slave to a Lucy? To anyone? Why follow blindly like a sheep? You were born to be an original.

An alternative to following is leading, even if no one is following, even if the crowd seems to be jeering.

Designer Robert L. Green says that the world has two types of people, the chic and the shriekers.

"The shriekers," he says, "are the copiers." The shriekers adopt "the language, the mannerisms, the hobbies, the rooms, the ways of dressing and living, of whomever they admire or envy. They are never the hunters, the discoverers, the originators, or the perfectionists. They are dependent on directions from others."

On the other hand, says Green, the chic "don't speak it or shriek it." They are "the copied, the criticized, and the envied." They possess the knack "of being able to do something with the same old money, space, or bodies. They are able to change the old because they can invent."

They have customized their style!

Cookie-Cutter Kids

While attending the Youth Fair in Miami recently, our family was caught up in a throng of teenagers. Thousands of them were milling about or huddled together in small groups.

I couldn't help but notice that each group looked identical to the other groups. I could hardly believe my eyes. All the girls had the same haircut, the same jeans, the same neon-colored shirt, the same brush sticking out of their hip pocket, the same lavender eyeshadow highlighted with yellow and pink. It was incredible.

When I mentioned this to Michelle, she said with a laugh, "They all look like they're cut out with a cookie cutter, don't they, Mom?" She was right, and that cookie-cutter look established their identity.

Some people call it "herd instinct." *Forbes* magazine ran an advertisement which read, "If you follow the herd, you may end up a pork-chop!" Dallas businesswoman Mary Crowley says a herd follower is, "vogue on the outside and vague on the inside!"

No matter what it's called, the desire for group acceptance affects "kids" of all ages. And it's not easy to break out of the mold. But I've found that by customizing my own style, by daring to be myself, I'm able to pass that same challenge along to my children.

One afternoon I overheard Michelle on the phone as she was telling her friend Lesli, "Everyone will be wearing jeans to the party. But I'm not. I'm wearing a skirt."

You may be saying, "No big deal," but in a way it was. To stand out when you're fourteen takes courage, and I complimented her. "Good for you, Honey, for choosing an outfit that *you* want to wear. You may start a trend!"

"Mother!" she gave me her withering look. "The day I start a trend will be the day."

"Well, you never know."

Off to the party she went, smiling and confident. I could tell she liked being different.

The Upstream Rafter

"The Road Not Taken" by Robert Frost is a favorite poem in our family, especially the lines,

> "Two roads diverged in a wood, and I—
>   I took the one less traveled by,
>   And that has made all the difference."*

I have spent a lot of time thinking about that road. Philosophers and poets laud it as the high and lofty road. Any common folk can ascend it and begin the journey, yet, not many choose "the road less traveled."

---

* Robert Frost, "The Road Not Taken," from *The Poetry of Robert Frost*, edited by Edward Connery Lathem. Copyright 1916, ©1969 by Holt Rinehart and Winston. Copyright 1944 Robert Frost. Reprinted by permission of Holt Rinehart and Winston, Publishers.

I sometimes picture mankind being swept downstream on a huge, rushing river, with thousands rafting swiftly by. Suddenly they see someone struggling and pushing against the current, straining to go *upstream* against all odds.

"Look at that nut!" they shout. "Stop her! Who does she think she is? That shouldn't be allowed. She's making waves!"

Any ol' person can float downstream. If you choose to go upstream against the flow, you may find yourself alone. Sounds a little scary, doesn't it? But at the same time you'll discover the fun in being who you were destined to be!

A Different Drumbeat

Michelle sat down for dinner one evening, and after several minutes of complete silence (a strange occurrence in itself), she suddenly announced, "You know, I've been thinking about what I want to do when I grow up. My father's a lawyer, my mother's an author, my sister wants to be a lawyer, and me—I want to be a singing telegramist!"

I seriously doubt if that will be her life's profession, but Michelle is marching to her own drumbeat. And while it's important that I customize my own style, it's equally important that I do not force my style on my children.

Many people are unhappy in their chosen walk of life because of parental coercion early in life.

A dentist told me, "My dad always regretted the fact that he didn't finish dental school, so I was forced to become a dentist just to satisfy his unfulfilled ambition. Do you know how I feel about dentistry? I hate it! Just hate it! Every day I hate it!"

How unfortunate. This man's life may be ruined. He not only hates his job, he probably hates his father, too. What a lesson to parents. Even if your child's goal does not seem as grand as yours, don't trample that dream or douse that spark. The fact that we all don't like the same things is what makes the world so exciting.

Recently I redecorated our hallway foyer by painting it sailor-blue and setting it off with a white table. The next day, one of my dearest friends came by to visit and remarked, "Marabel, I have to tell you," she said gently, "I really don't like the color of that blue."

Just for a second a pang went through me like an arrow of rejection, and then I felt secure. I grinned and said, "I understand. It's strong. But I love it." End of conversation.

Expressing yourself is a statement about who you are. Sometimes a little courage is required.

Carolyn Lewis, writing for *Newsweek,* compared her New York City life with that of her two sons in Maine. When her sons moved out of The Big Apple, her friends looked down on them, almost in pity.

A year later, she compared their different lifestyles. "For my sons there is, of course, the rural bounty of fresh-grown vegetables, line-caught fish, and the shared riches of neighbors' orchards and gardens. There is the unpaid babysitter for whose children my daughter-in-law babysits in return, and neighbors who barter their skills and labor.

"I, by comparison," she wrote, "living in my overpriced city apartment, walking to work past putrid sacks of street garbage, paying usurious taxes to local and state governments I generally abhor, I am rated middle class!"

So who is to be pitied? Not the one set apart by location or type of work, but the one who is caught in the downstream and can't escape. Or won't.

Don't copy the copies. You are an original. Show your own label.

CUSTOMIZE YOUR BODY

The third area I've learned to customize is my body. A poll taken recently among teenage girls revealed that their number one problem was their body. All other runner-up problems—boys, money, boys, career, boys, parents, drugs, and more boys—were not nearly as important.

If that same poll were given to women over twenty, do you think their number one problem would also be their body? If not number one, I'll bet it would be high on the list. How else do you explain the billions spent on plastic surgery, spas, beauty parlors, boutiques, color charts, health clubs, and diet centers?

No wonder we're concerned about our body. It is the "house" we live in. Wherever we go, the house goes with us.

What do we know about it? Let's check it out.

• *You have only one.* No more. No less. No trade-ins or exchanges allowed by management as long as we're here on Planet Earth.

• *Each body is unique.* No one else's is quite like yours, not even your identical twin's. You are the Designer's original.

• *Inventory control is precise.* Your Maker not only knows your name and your needs, but according to Luke 12, He even keeps track of the number of hairs on your head. Authorities tell us that blondes have about 145,000 hairs, dark-haired people have 120,000, and redheads have 90,000 hairs, more or less. Talk about special!

• *Certain features are unchangeable.* Take skin color and voice and height for instance. Once you're full grown, if you are four feet or five feet or seven feet, that's it, baby. There's no more adding or subtracting. So it does no good to whine about your size or to lose sleep if you don't have Cheryl Tiegs' legs or Christie Brinkley's body. Someone else will always be prettier and younger. The challenge is to make the very best of what *you* have.

• *Other parts are changeable.* That is, you can control certain factors—your posture and your shape (somewhat) and your weight (especially weight). By self-control or lack of it, you can improve your body or abuse it. The choice is up to you, although the results may be evident to the rest of the world.

• *Service affects operation.* Each body, like a piece of machinery, operates most efficiently under certain optimum conditions. Take your car, for example. It runs best when the engine is perfectly tuned up, tires aligned, and the vehicle driven smoothly.

And it's just the same with this vehicle called your body. It is designed to operate most efficiently under certain conditions, ideal weight range, muscle tone, pulse rate, and so on.

We all have a pretty good idea what our ideal weight should be, even if it's tough to admit at times.

What is that for you? When was the last time you were at that weight? Not since the third grade, you say? (Now, who am I to meddle? Actually, I'm talking to myself. I just had my 10,000–mile checkup. I'm so out of shape that I need a retread. I start my program tomorrow!)

The Incredible Hunk

Meanwhile, back at the kitchen sink and tonight's dinner. Isn't it too bad we can't cut out food cold-turkey?

Why is the lure of the chocolate cake stronger than my strength to resist? Or if you're single, does the call of the doughnut have more appeal than the opinion of that gorgeous hunk down the street? Does the doughnut blot out all sense of reason? Why must you have that doughnut right now?

The sad fact is, the doughnut's gone in two minutes and the taste doesn't even linger. It doesn't satisfy. You still want another.

But the harm has been done, 'cause there it is, following right along "behind." Any appetite out of control is counterproductive, totally detrimental. It ruins chances for other victories. And as the appetite increases, so does the frustration.

Are all appetites created equal? Is Connie Calorie's appetite for chocolate mousse any greater than the skinny model's? Don't you think it's just as difficult for Skinny to eat only three bites of mousse and put down her spoon, as it would be for Connie to do the same? But instead, Connie goes back for seconds and on the way looks at Skinny and says, "You're so skinny, it's disgusting. You never had a problem in the first place!"

Oh really? When Brooke Shields passes a candy store, does the temptation bother her as much as it does you and me? I'll bet it does. Has to. The question is not, "Is there an urge?" but rather, "How has she learned to control it?"

Six Slender Secrets of Fashion Models

Occasionally I have lunch with beautiful, rail-thin models, and I always make it a point to observe their eating habits, especially when there are 10,000 luscious calories being placed within easy reach.

I asked some of these ravishing beauties what drives them to keep slender. I wanted to know not only how they got it off, but how they are able to keep it off.

Here are some of their time-tested beauty secrets, plus a few of my own (for whatever they're worth).

1. *Explode the "Clean Plate Syndrome."*

Many Americans have been taught from early childhood to clean their plates at every meal. One woman told me that when she was a little girl, it was the unpardonable sin at her house to leave anything on the plate—not even a spoonful of cereal, applesauce, or mashed potatoes. So at breakfast when her mother wasn't looking, she would dump uneaten oatmeal into her pocket. (Imagine her reaching into that pocket for a pencil during math class!)

In urging our children to eat their green beans and other nutritious food not necessarily to their liking, we parents often become the world's worst manipulators. We use every excuse under the sun to justify force-feeding our kids.

• *Guilt.* This is the worst of all. "Millions are dying in India, Howard. Now, eat your corn!"

• *Reward.* "If you don't eat your squash, you won't get any dessert." Holding dessert out as a reward only compounds the problem by encouraging a dessert every meal and a dependency on sweets.

• *Health.* Miss Nutrition speaking, "You want to be healthy, don't you? Now finish those lima beans. There are four grams of potassium in the pile that's left."

- *Hurt Feelings.* You've heard this one. "Daddy worked so hard all week to pay for that spinach, and he feels so bad when you don't appreciate what he did for you."

- *Good Manners.* "A good little girl always cleans her plate. Never forget that!" (Now who would want to be a bad little girl who leaves food on her plate)?

- *Fear.* When we were first married Charlie and I lived next door to a young divorcee with a two-year-old hyperactive little tot. We were awakened every morning at 6:00 A.M. with a blood-curdling scream that came right through our bedroom wall, "Eat your eggy! Eat it! Eat it! Eat it!" (I've often wondered where that kid is today).

- *Permission to Play.* And who hasn't heard (or used) this one, "You're not leaving this table until you eat every last bite on your plate!"

When I was only nine, five extra bites of potatoes didn't have much effect on my figure. But today as a mother of two, I find that those last few bites of linguini, hot garlic rolls, or chocolate torte do make a difference. They combine with the Law of Gravity to head South, finding a home just below my waistline. And because of my early conditioning, it is difficult to leave even one bite on my plate. Usually wild horses can't keep me from eating it. But, just knowing that I don't *have* to eat the last bite of everything in sight helps take the pressure off . . . and the pounds.

2. *Pick and Play.*

My friend Sunny is a slim, well-built blonde. She is a model from Las Vegas, and when she walks into a restaurant she draws stares from men and women alike.

Recently I sat next to Sunny at a charity luncheon. I had to psych myself up and spend extra prep time before daring to meet her. The luncheon was one of those all-day killers with speeches, dessert, fashion show, and raffle.

I found myself bloated by the end of the pasta course, but I forced myself to keep on eating. (After all, I had paid for it, I might as well get my money's worth, right? That's false-economy logic.)

As we chatted, I wondered how Sunny managed to keep her perfect figure perfect. She attends lavish parties at least once a day. How come she's not a blimp?

When the Chicken Breast Veronica arrived smothered in cream sauce, I thought, "If she puts that away, I want to see where it goes."

Well, first of all, it went very slowly. Sunny just nibbled. She tasted without pigging out. She enjoyed with moderation.

Then she played with the food that remained. While appearing to be eating, she was actually only moving it around her plate. The stuffed tomato was shifted behind the grapes. Part of the chicken slid under the parsley. The grapes got buried in cream sauce.

I continued to watch as Sunny made little swirls in the cream sauce all in a counterclockwise direction. I was certain that none of the other girls at the table were aware of what she was doing. She appeared to be enjoying her lunch as much as anyone. She tasted almost everything, but finished almost nothing.

She left the luncheon with her dynamic figure intact. I left with a full stomach and a super tip for my next big meal out—pick and play. No one will ever know but you!

3. *Think Thin.*

What gives these skinny fashion models the will power to resist the pastry tray that does me in every time?

I asked Barbara, another model, this question. "How do you do it?"

"Simple," she replied. "It's just a matter of priorities. On the one hand I've got an urge for sweets (who doesn't?), but on the other hand, I've got to keep my eye on the greater goal—my modeling career. If I let my appetite run wild for a day or so, I'm in big trouble."

So *that's* the secret—keep your eye on the greater goal. That goal may include a career, or that good-looking guy you've been eyeing, or your own health, or the personal satisfaction that comes from looking trim.

When food's an issue I struggle between the desire for it and the desire for approbation. One pulls at my stomach and the other pulls at my heart, and I'm wrenched in the middle.

One of my most difficult times comes when I face a huge buffet. I am tempted to eat until I drop or explode, whichever comes first. But I have learned to set my limit *in advance*. Otherwise I'd clean the entire table!

Try it; it works. It really does help to think thin, *before* the cheesecake arrives.

4. *Pig Out in Public.*

This is applicable when you can't control that "urge to splurge." Let me tell you my reasoning.

I'm a closet eater. That doesn't mean I eat closets, or, for that matter, that I eat in closets. But when I'm feeling blue, I sneak a snack when no one's looking.

Last month I had a pity party. I was upset and nervous and feeling sorry for myself. In my hyper state, I only wanted to eat, alone. That night, after everyone was asleep, I tiptoed to the kitchen. I fixed a peanut butter and jelly sandwich (another great weakness) and a glass of milk. Guilty (and stuffed), I tossed and turned all night.

The next morning I made a resolution for this year: Pig out in public, and only in public. I will not allow myself to gorge in secret. When I do, I'm only kidding myself. The very reason I want to eat in secret is (a) I don't need to eat then at all, and (b) the food I eat is usually the junk food I shouldn't be eating.

5. If Only?

One of life's great frustrations comes not from comparing myself to others, but comparing myself to what I could be. If I know I could be thin, but I see a baby blimp in the mirror, that's frustration. Knowing I'm capable of more is what hurts.

The key words are "capable of more." Are you? I know that I am. How can I honestly say that I live up to the maximum potential to which the Lord has blessed me?

I often wonder, "If only . . ." And apparently others have too.

The runner who lost the race when she was five pounds overweight will always wonder—if only . . .

And the Dallas housewife who lost her husband of thirteen years when she was twenty-four pounds overweight. If only . . .

And the saleswoman who failed to receive her promotion when she was twenty-one pounds overweight. If only . . .

Regardless of what diet you may choose, only two things are necessary to lose weight. One, a desire to lose it, and two, a willingness to change your lifestyle in order to accomplish it.

Why not make your "if only" come true?

6. *Move It.*

Everybody, but everybody is jogging in Miami. A steady stream of joggers pours out of side streets, slowing traffic, causing near misses (depending on what brief attire female joggers are modeling), and generally causing guilt feelings for those standing on the curb.

I had a mental block against jogging just because everybody was doing it. But I couldn't help but notice my friend the model and her firm fanny in tight jeans. Slowly I began to toy with the idea. Maybe . . . just maybe, it could help.

The first night that I donned my shorts and Nikes and ran down the driveway was a monumental moment. I was stunned to discover that at the end of the driveway (which is about nine yards), I was gasping for breath.

What a shock! Dejected, I thought of retiring from my new jogging program before I had even begun. Just then a neighbor walked by and asked, "How's it going?"

"I'm about ready to quit," I panted.

"You don't quit, Marabel," she remarked and strolled on down the road. Bless that lady. She doesn't know what she did for me. What a grand record to play over in your brain, "You don't quit!"

I decided that she was absolutely right. The next night I made it down the driveway and halfway up the block. Now, years later I'm running (and that's a loose term—Michelle's cat walks faster than I jog) at least three miles every other night. I even ran in a mini-marathon last year. The entire pack of runners left me in the dust and I finished dead last. But what a feeling of exhilaration!

Jogging has become our family pursuit in the evenings. Charlie flies by, lost in whatever he's hearing through his stereo headphones, strengthening his heart and trimming his body. My girls seem to glide above the pavement. I love the feeling of family as we work out together.

I realize that the thought of jogging may not especially thrill you. But consider this. Medical science shows that even if you cut back drastically on calories, you still may not lose weight because your metabolism has slowed down to live with your calorie intake.

Horrors! Trapped in a fat body, and not eating won't cure it?

One answer, of course, is exercise. If not jogging, how about walking? Or perhaps an aerobics class?

When I signed up for a class the first time, it was an intimidating experience. Seventeen leotards filled with varying lumps and shapes were kicking, twisting, bending, and stretching. I was right there in the midst of them with beads of sweat on the end of my nose.

But it was fun. We even smiled at times (like when we finally collapsed on the mat at the end of twenty-five minutes).

And this kind of exercise didn't make me feel so alone in my battle. In fact, I felt rather encouraged because I could always find a rear or pair of thighs that were bigger than mine. I tried harder, I kicked higher.

And then, finally, came the sweet fruit of my labors. After a few weeks, I could tell a difference. The buttoned skirt didn't cut off circulation. My face really did glow, and maybe best of all, I felt energetic and eager to face each morning.

What is your thing? Is it jogging or aerobic dancing or swimming? Remember, we are all at different stages on this exercise road.

If you're not ready to run a marathon, don't dismay. If you merely stand instead of sit, that may be progress. But, your body needs to be pushed. Exert a little energy, work up a sweat. You may hate it while you're doing it, but afterwards comes the reward.

The bottom line for your bottom is, "Move it!"

EMERGENCY CHECK LIST WHEN ALL ELSE FAILS

1. Weigh before eating. (Don't be deceived by a temporary weight "loss." A pound is not lost unless it remains lost for three days.)
2. Brush after eating.
3. Weigh after brushing (especially after a pig-out. Force yourself to look at the scale).
4. Fill up with stuffers (rabbit food).
5. Call a buddy (accountability helps).
6. Take small portions on small plates and eat small bites slowly.
7. Put away the box before eating the "last" bite.
8. Don't buy clothes to fit a larger size.
9. Reach for your mate instead of your plate (dietetic).
10. Don't grocery shop on an empty stomach.
11. Don't cook on an empty stomach.
12. Don't eat on an empty stomach.
13. Take a cold shower.

2

CLEANSE

Have you ever started worrying in the middle of the night and then couldn't get back to sleep? One night a few weeks ago, I awoke and my heart was filled with despair. I tossed and turned.

All sorts of ghosts danced before me—Betty Bitter, Gilda Guilt-Trip, Perry Noid, Phoebe Phobia, Harriet Habit, Pierre Pressure.

As I stared at each one, all kinds of emotions went through my head. My downer chart was going berserk, like a pinball machine with bells and lights flashing.

Finally I couldn't stand it any longer. Sleep was impossible. I climbed out of bed and went to the living room with pad and pencil ready to do battle with these culprits. I began to write down all the things that were bothering me. The biggies were first. And then the lesser problems. Just putting them down was a relief in itself.

Then I suddenly realized a very startling fact—most of

these ghosts were conceived in my past. They related to some past action in my life.

So why was I allowing my past to control me? If I allowed it, my past could ruin my future. These were some downers I *could* control.

1. Bury Betty Bitter and Friends

Betty Bitter had climbed aboard the week before when I was ripped off by a sewing machine salesman through a newspaper ad. The machine didn't work when I got it home and I was mad. Mad over the time wasted driving across town twice. Mad over the money lost. Mad at the man because he wouldn't fix the machine or refund the money or return my old machine ("It's already sold!" he said).

So Betty Bitter was a past-tenser, yet her spirit lived on.

This particular night Betty and friends arrived together—jumping up and down on my bed. They wouldn't leave no matter what. They were uninvited guests who brought bad news.

Like a bad-news telegram, Betty Bitter started out, "Remember when . . .?" She had returned again to haunt, and I knew that she planned to stay.

After I had identified each of these rude intruders and listed all the problems under each one, I looked over my list. Many of them were Betty Bitter's burdens. She dredged up bitter memories—the times of high anxiety, angry confrontations, childhood disappointments, and shattered dreams, all of them swirling around in the middle of the night. Her list

Phoebe Phobia

Betty Bitter

Pierre Pressure

Gilda Guilt-Trip

Harriet Habit

Candy Cant

Perry Noid

Patty Pity

Nellie Not Tonight

Taiwan On

was the longest and she was screaming the loudest, so I decided to deal with her first.

In desperation I prayed to God, "The past is gone. I am not going to let it control me or destroy me. Forgive me, Lord, for my anger. I give my past to you."

A calm fell over me, and at last, sweet sleep came.

This ghost of Betty Bitter had come and gone. Amazingly the other ghosts left with her. I suppose they moved on to another unsuspecting, sleepless victim.

It is never easy dealing with Betty Bitter. She's one tough cookie to shake. But it can be done. Little by little we can learn to control the way our past affects us today.

The Mad Hater

When Laura and Michelle were small, we sometimes watched TV together. I remember one particular episode of "Sesame Street" where the little animated figure, Roosevelt Franklin, saw someone he despised across the street. He shook violently and shouted,

> When I am walking down the street
> And there's a bad guy that I meet,
> It makes me mad,
>   Very angry,
>   Very, very angry.
> It makes me mad.

Roosevelt didn't have a corner on anger. As I was growing up, I saw firsthand the result of Betty Bitter gone mad, in the person of my own mother.

Her "hate list" was full and overflowing with people who had wronged her—the ones who had ripped her off, and double-crossed her, and talked behind her back. She was consumed with anger toward each one.

It all started when I was about six. One of my aunts came to stay with us. She lived in a weird and mystical world. She held séances in my playroom, and called back the spirits of long-departed loved ones. She had great control over my mother. This aunt talked incessantly to a spirit named Dr. White who perched on her shoulder. My stepfather couldn't stand her (or Dr. White).

Occasionally there was relief from the strange goings-on in my house. I remember one Thanksgiving Day when I was eight. Several of my aunts and uncles came to visit.

My cousins and I played Hide-and-Seek in the backyard. I was giddy. I loved the laughter and shouting and loud conversation.

But that was the first and last celebration that I can remember. During the day someone crossed my mother, and that was the end. No more dinner parties. In fact, no one was invited over again for anything.

Once, two of my aunts knocked at the front door. My mother screamed at them and actually kicked them. She threatened to call the police. My aunts didn't get past the front door. (We weren't a real close family.)

Our neighbors and friends didn't have a chance either. In some way each one had wronged my mother, so there was no one left worthy of her presence.

My stepfather tried to intercede on behalf of the relatives and friends, but that put him in big trouble. He was labeled "on their side," and so from then on, he was an enemy, too.

My mother started divorce proceedings and went to bed

(I'm still not sure of that connection), where she stayed for six long years, nursing her grievances. When I came home from school each day, I sat in her room, mainly out of loneliness, while she reiterated the injustices she had suffered.

She had no apparent physical problems, but she had become ill from her inner torment. At the end of the six years, my stepfather died (still undivorced), and she got out of bed.

But my mother was still "closed down" and our house was closed to the outside world. It seemed to me that I lived in darkness.

Going to school each morning meant freedom. Outside was sunlight. I couldn't wait to run out the door and up the street. I felt like I was released from prison. Going to classes, I forgot about home until I once again reached my street.

Walking up the gravel driveway and forcing myself to go into that house each evening took great determination, but I had no place else to go. When I entered the back door, oppression came over me like a blanket. The atmosphere was suffocating. I could hardly breathe.

No one knew the desperation I felt. I didn't dare bring a friend to this strange, dark house.

By the time I was a senior I felt like I'd go crazy if I didn't escape. Thoughts of turning on the gas or slitting my wrists constantly plagued me, but I wanted to *live,* not die. I bided my time, working after school, saving my money, knowing that when I turned eighteen, my mother couldn't legally bring me back.

Finally the day came. I packed my few belongings and sneaked out of the house. A friend drove me to the YWCA. The rent was eight dollars a week. Tips from my job at The Tea Room would barely cover living expenses.

I called to tell my mother where I was. Frantic and furious, she screamed that I would never make it and that one day I would come crawling back to her for help. As I write these words my heart weeps for the anguish I caused her. But for me it was a matter of life or death.

Never mind eating peanut butter and crackers three meals a day. Never mind not having pretty clothes and shoes. Never mind being alone and fighting fear, loneliness, and guilt.

I was eighteen and strong. I would make it.

2. Release Your Grip

Today my mother continues to live in her fantasy world, reliving like a broken record the "wrongs" done to her. She refuses to let them go. She refuses to forgive or forget. Her life is no life. She is eaten up with the past, which is twisted and warped. To my knowledge she has no friends, no social life. She sits at home with the blinds still drawn.

For over twenty-four years I have not seen my mother. She refuses to see me or her grandchildren. How sad. Such a waste. A living example of bitterness gone wild.

Not only does her family suffer because of the alienation, but also society loses a productive person. As Eli Weisel, survivor of the Auschwitz prison camp, wrote, "Wherever hatred exists, the hater suffers more than the hated, but both suffer, and so does society."

My childhood experience is a warning to me. I know that I, too, could turn into a hermit like my mother. And if I hold on to my hurts and refuse to forgive, my heart also could become bitter.

What is the alternative to anger? Isn't it better (and easier in the long run) to acknowledge it and give it up to the Lord?

I realize that this is a foreign concept to some women. Just yesterday over lunch, a friend agonized over her divorce. She said, "My therapist told me to *release* my hatred. I don't know what that means."

I told her, "I believe you can't really release it or let go of it in your own strength. Ask God to help you let it go, because then He's in charge. Ultimately He'll settle accounts—for you and your ex-husband. He'll bring about justice.

"But look what happens otherwise," I explained. "Without God in the picture, *you* must administer justice, which of course you can't do, and so you are consumed by your own emotions."

I suggested a little exercise. "Clench your fist. Imagine your husband inside, with all the pain he has caused you. Now squeeze it hard. Then slowly open up your fingers and give your husband and the pain over to the Lord. Let it go. Release it. Be free of the past. Don't let it rob you of life."

Does the past have a stranglehold on you? Do you love to rehash trash? Does it do any good? Do you notice that your friends move away when you start to unload? When you look in the mirror, do you wonder, "Who's that angry witch staring at me?"

On your Line of Life, those past bitter memories cause *new* negative emotions every time you think of them. It's a vicious repetition, and who needs it? There is far too much adventure awaiting you *today* to be cluttered up with the past.

When any bitter memory comes floating by, I say to

myself, "Enough! You have already repeated it 17,000 times. Run it by one more time if you must, savor it, and then lay it to rest."

What a feeling! What a cleansing when I release my bitterness.

3. HEAL THE MEMORIES

A tour guide in Nashville was telling a group of students how the South won the Civil War. "Just a minute," one girl interrupted. "I thought the *North* won this thing."

"Not while I'm tour guide, they didn't!" he snapped.

He had a long memory. And don't we all? We all seem to justify our prejudices. Psychologist James Mallory says that we each have a Hall of Injustice that we love to visit.

We reserve the hall for special enemies we can't forget. We invite friends in, "Come into my museum and see my statues, my villains. Now here's Fred. Let me tell you how he did me wrong." His statue is polished and shining from constant handling.

Such is the case of my friend who continually relives her divorce blow by blow. All she can remember (and it's been five years since they divorced) are the faults of her husband. She blots out the *pleasant* memories of the past as though they never happened.

She has set up her own Hall of Injustice. Every time she thinks of her ex, it's another negative, just like a ghost of the past coming to haunt her. Think of it—self-induced misery for five long years.

And guess who's the loser? Not her ex, but herself. He probably never even thinks of her, but she is still controlled by him. She is not free. Even worse, her body takes the toll.

Already she is beginning to experience some of the side effects of anger—depression, high blood pressure, and migraine headaches.

Your memories, like hers, may be painful, and your scars may be deep. You may need much prayer and perhaps even professional counseling to help you overcome them. But there can be a healing of those painful memories.

Remember that haunting theme song from *The Way We Were,* as Barbra Streisand and Robert Redford separated for the last time? We need to remember the laughter, the cherished memories, and forget those "too painful to remember."

No matter who you are, or where you are, or what you've done, don't despair. More important than the way you were is the way you can be.

And what about your Hall of Injustice? Isn't it time for a bonfire? Burn it down today.

Say good-bye to Betty (and her friends Patty Pity and Gilda Guilt-Trip). Beat it, ghosts!

3

CHALLENGE

The letter from a South Carolina housewife began, "Help. Tell me how to handle Rodney. If you can show me a way to cope, you can save another marriage. Please hurry."

The letter continued, "I am giving you a list of just some of Rodney's faults, so you can see what I have to put up with."

RODNEY'S FAULTS

1. Puts people down, even those he doesn't know.
2. Brags on himself.
3. Gets mad when he pays the bills.
4. Never says anything nice about anyone.
5. Throws his clothes everywhere.
6. His end-table stays messy.
7. Sex is the only important thing to him.

---

8. His mouth is the reason we're never invited to anyone's house.
9. Butts in when someone's talking.
10. Has a snide remark when someone says something.
11. Gets right nasty-mouthed if I don't feel like sex.
12. Gets upset if I go anywhere.

I can list more. The list just goes on and on. See what I mean?

Trouble in South Carolina

I don't know anyone who doesn't have troubles of some kind. Whether you're from South Carolina or South Korea, if you're breathing, you've got troubles. For this lady, her biggest problem seems to be Rodney. Yours may be far more serious than hers, but who's to judge another's problem? For South Carolina, it's serious.

When problems come (and we know they will), how can we deal with them and still keep our sanity? And better yet, how can we convert them from negatives to positives?

Here are six tips on how to turn your downers into uppers.

1. FACE FACTS SQUARELY

Our close friend, Dr. Everett Sugarbaker, is a cancer surgeon in Miami. He photographs the affected part of each patient's body prior to surgery. Then he photographs the patient again after the operation.

I had an opportunity to look at some slides he had prepared for a medical lecture. One almost did me in. It showed a lady in her thirties who was completely eaten by cancer. Her swollen body was an entire mass of sores. The picture was utterly grotesque. I could hardly bear to look at it.

I asked the doctor, "Why did she wait so long before coming in?"

"She didn't want to admit she had cancer," he answered sadly. "She was denying to herself that she had the disease and waited until she was beyond help."

This problem of denial is not only limited to a frightened cancer patient. It is also a favorite technique for anyone who doesn't want to face facts.

Not long ago, I saw a bumper sticker that read, "The surest way to mishandle a problem is to avoid facing it."

All humans love to rationalize and blame others for their actions and mistakes. Refusal to accept blame is denial in all its glory. And the underlying problem remains unattended.

An example of *not* facing facts squarely was reported in the *Toronto Sun*. The excuses given to insurance adjusters by drivers involved in accidents were classic:

- "To avoid hitting the bumper of the car in front, I struck the pedestrian."

- "A truck backed through my windshield into my wife's face."

- "A pedestrian hit me and went under my car."

- "The guy was all over the road; I had to swerve a number of times before I hit him."

- "I pulled away from the side of the road, glanced at my mother-in-law and headed over the embankment."

- "I was on my way to the doctor with rear-end trouble when my universal joint gave way, causing me to have an accident."

Problems, if ignored, usually don't go away. In fact, they often get bigger. As our pastor, Steve Brown, said one Sunday, "When you are confronted by a lion, you either make friends with him, or you get eaten."

What is the greatest problem facing you today? Is it your husband or your children or your doctor's report? Maybe it's your weight or your finances? Don't deny the reality. Identify it, and face it as a problem. Only then can you begin to deal with it.

2. ANALYZE YOUR ALTERNATIVES

Back to our friend from South Carolina—the housewife with the expanding list of "One Dozen Things Wrong with Rodney." What are her alternatives? As I see it, she only has three.

(1) *She can ditch Rodney.*

The knee-jerk inclination is to split. The song, "Fifty Ways to Leave Your Lover," describes the quick fix:

You just slip out the back, Jack.
    Make a new plan, Stan.
You don't need to be coy, Roy.
    Just get yourself free.

Hop on the bus, Gus.
    You don't need to discuss much.
Just drop off the key, Lee.
    And get yourself free.

Sounds so simple, doesn't it? But that's not what she wanted. She closed the letter with, "P.S. I don't want a divorce. I love Rodney and he's a wonderful father, but I just wish he would change some of these things."

So now what?

(2) *She can stick and stew.*

A second alternative is to stick with the marriage and stew about it. This is Ms. Martyr. Anyone can spot her a mile away, especially her husband. This is probably the most miserable of all the alternatives.

Why? Because the problem doesn't remain constant; it usually gets worse. Or rather, Rodney usually gets worse. Her list of his wrongs will never again be twelve. It will grow daily and will soon be the size of a Manhattan phone book.

(3) *She can accept his quirks.*

A third solution is possible if Troubled wants to keep her marriage. How? By changing her attitude toward Rodney.

This will probably be the challenge of her life, but if she wins, she will be forever grateful for initiating the change.

I can already hear screams around the room over this suggestion. "What do you mean? Do you want her to keep on living with that creep?"

Well, remember that she has already ruled out the divorce option herself. She is living in Option #2 as a whiner. But she's miserable. So what's left? Option #3 is simply another alternative.

Let's look at Rodney's problems. Are they all that unusual? Anyone who has ever lived with another person could probably make a similar list. In fact, someone with a list of only twelve would be the ideal mate for many.

Marriage involves accepting the differences in your mate. That includes all of his quirks, however strange they may seem.

The Dirt-Free Diet

I read in the *New York Times* recently about a housewife who loves to eat dirt. That's right. She is Fannie Glasser of

Cruger, Mississippi, and her thing is dirt—good, old, rich, and delicious dirt. "When it's good and dug from the right place," she said, "dirt has a fine sour taste."

At the time Mrs. Glasser was interviewed, she was on a dirt-free diet, but she admitted, "There are times when I really miss it. I wish I had some dirt right now."

Talk about quirks! Can you imagine Mr. Glasser's reaction when he comes home from a long day at work, starved to death and asks, "What's for dinner tonight, hon?" just as Fannie walks in from the garden with a pail!

Who doesn't have quirks? We all do. Your personality is the sum of all your quirks, and that's what sets you apart from the rest of the world (and sometimes, even from your husband as well!).

According to "Your Marriage Personality Test" by Jessie R. Runner, in *Your Life* magazine, all personalities are divided into two main types, called the *R's* and *Z's*.

The *R* wants "to live *regularly* according to a planned *routine.*" He (or she) makes *rites* of doing things at the *right time* in the *right place* in the *right way*. An *R* is *reserved* in friendships; he believes in *restraining* one's impulses and sometimes tries to *restrain* others as well.

The *Z* on the other hand is impulsive and generous and spontaneous. He (or she) works with *zest* and *zeal*, rather than methodically.

When you compare the words *regular, routine, reserved,* and *restrained* with *zest, zeal, zip,* and *zowie,* you can see the difference between these two personality types.

But do you know who the *R* usually picks out to marry? You guessed it! The opposite, the *Z*, who is miserable if caught in a round of routine details.

This was certainly true with Charlie and me. He was pure

R and I was pure *Z*. But some of his *R* traits that I admired before marriage began to irritate me afterwards.

For example, when it came to money matters, he held on to his money. I was dismayed to discover the underlying foundation of a pure *R*—the reason Charlie had money to spend is because he spent no money! He was *retentive*.

Charlie was also having second thoughts about me. Before marriage, he had been intrigued by my enthusiasm. But afterwards my zip, zest, and zowie approach to life drove him crazy. And money? Saving money meant nothing to me. I thought money was to spend!

Before marriage, opposites attract. After marriage, they often repel.

What are your husband's or friend's quirks that drive you up the wall? Have you been trying for years to change these?

Marriage is not so much a matter of "finding compatibles," wrote columnist Sydney J. Harris, "as it is finding compatible incompatibles—of recognizing and accepting those particular kinds of defects in a mate that do not upset one's basic equilibrium."

Compatible incompatibles can function as a team, a support team for each other, and they can bond together in love for a common purpose.

If that's not true in your marriage, what are your alternatives? To split, or to stew, or to start a change that just might save your marriage? The choice is yours.

A lady told me, "One evening I tried your suggestion about accepting my husband's quirks. At the dinner table, instead of nagging him about his sloppy eating habits, I bragged about his softball team. He lit up like a 100-watt bulb. I did too!"

Try it. Brag instead of nag. You, too, may end up with an electric husband!

3. PUT THE PROBLEM IN PERSPECTIVE

Albert Einstein was once asked to define *relativity*. He replied, "When you sit with a nice girl for two hours, you think that it's only a minute. But when you sit on a hot stove for a minute, you think it's two hours! That's relativity!"

I asked my neighbor, "How do you feel?"

"Compared to what?" she asked.

What an important question—compared to what? Two weeks is only fourteen days, but how much shorter it seems when you're on vacation than when you're on a diet.

Early in our marriage, Charlie and I had a fight that blew itself all out of proportion. I thought for sure it was the end of love. I remember running into the bedroom and crying, wondering if our marriage would make it.

Looking back, I can't even tell you what the problem was. I am sure that it was something worth fighting for, but I honestly can't remember what.

Isn't that the way with so many of our problems? At first they seem enormous, but four days later, they're gone and new problems have taken their place. That's why, when downers hit, it's so important to keep them in perspective, always keeping in mind the larger picture.

Steve Clinton is professor at the Campus Crusade International School of Theology. Dr. Clinton lived on the outskirts of the San Bernardino Forest which caught fire several years ago.

Just as he returned home for lunch one day, he noticed that a part of the wood-shingle roof was on fire. Quickly he climbed up a ladder with a water hose to extinguish the flames. As he climbed onto the roof, he felt fire burning the shingles right underneath his feet. He jumped back, lost his balance, and fell off the roof.

No time to think about injuries, he raced to the front of the house, just as his wife, Virginia, had run outside with one-year-old Shanna. The family stood together on the lawn and watched the house collapse in flames within a matter of moments. Other homes in the neighborhood were also on fire, and the flames were spreading as the Clintons drove through the flaming debris to safety. Two hundred and eighty others would also lose their homes that day.

Weeks later Dr. Clinton described how he felt as he watched all of his earthly possessions destroyed, including wedding pictures, family scrapbooks, and his newly completed manuscript.

"I was just so grateful that my wife and children were out of the house," he told me. "That's all I cared about. A few minutes more and they would have been trapped inside."

The Clintons have life in perspective.

Whenever there is trouble it helps to see the whole picture. As Paul Harvey says, "In times like these, it helps to know that there have always been times like these."

What is your deepest downer today? No matter how awful it seems, try looking at it from another perspective—the ultimate perspective. How reassuring to know that in the end, God is sovereign and will make everything right for those who love Him and are called according to His purpose.

Phil Driscoll, Grammy Award winner and former trumpeter with the rock group "Blood, Sweat and Tears," gives this sure-fire word of encouragement, "Read the end of *The Book,* man! God's already won!"

4. Turn Worry into Action

Have you ever planned an outdoor picnic and then couldn't sleep for a week wondering whether it would rain on that day? That's worry. Even though you can't do a thing about the weather, you allow it to control you. Worry is fretting the upsetting. Worry is preoccupation over circumstances you can't control.

One reason we worry is that we fail to make contingency plans. Often it's possible to control future events simply by taking some action now. For example, if weather is so important to the success of the picnic, maybe you could arrange for an alternate site. Or check out rent-a-tent prices. Pass out umbrellas. Make it a pool party. Schedule a rain-out date. At least, the options will help diffuse the worry.

Worry isn't consumed with yesterdays. Worry is a future fear—a negative, a downer that clouds your day and robs you of joy and strength. It's an energy drainer.

I don't know about you, but all those electrical impulses coming at me all day long make me *tired.* Just customizing my life and cleaning out the ghosts leave me exhausted. My motivation evaporates like the dew in the morning, and I come to a screeching halt. So when I run out of steam, I pull out my Worry Defuser—a simple three-question exercise to help turn my worries into action.

1. What are my three most pressing problems?
2. If wishing would do it, what do I wish would happen in each case?
3. What action am I going to take to make those wishes come true?

This is what it looks like on paper.

WORRY DEFUSER		
Three Pressing Problems	What I Wish Would Happen	Action I Will Take
1.		
2.		
3.		

Whenever I work this little exercise I keep the paper in a prominent position on my desk, so that at a glance I can see where I'm going. When the problems swirling around in my head are identified and put down on paper, my mind is freed of confusion.

This exercise also helps start my motor. If I wait for someone to light a fire under me, I may have a long wait. Life is too short to waste even a minute. I must be my own self-starter.

Worry paralyzes action, but action is worry that has started to move. If you need to put motion to your worry, try the Worry-Defuser exercise. Get going. Take a step. Light a match.

Oh, and one more word. Do you know that most of the things we worry about probably will never come to pass anyway? I was reminded of this one night when Michelle prayed, "Oh Lord, thank you that today was not nearly as bad as I thought it would be."

In a similar vein, that wise old sage Mark Twain once reflected, "I'm an old man. I've had many problems, most of which never happened!"

The Law of Averages is on your side, so "The Worst Case" scenario probably will not happen (unless your name is Murphy!).

5. THINK "PRO-ACTIVE," NOT "RE-ACTIVE"

The Chinese word for crisis is made up of two characters: *danger* and *opportunity*. The optimist sees opportunity in every danger; the pessimist sees danger in every opportunity.

My normal reaction to a problem is panic. I tend to sink immediately under the load. But instead of "re-acting" negatively, I can be "pro-active." I can take positive action rather than respond with the normal negative reaction. Often this means anticipating the problem and taking action to avoid it *before* it happens.

By being pro-active I can see the problem as an opportunity. W.B. Prescott recognized, "We are all continually faced with a series of great opportunities brilliantly disguised as insoluble problems."

What a wonderful way of looking at it! When troubles come, I can greet them as opportunities, "Oh, hi there, I've been expecting you!" But I have discovered it's necessary to decide on a positive mindset *before* trouble comes. Then as Scripture says, I'll be able to "stand firm" and "let nothing move" me.

I encourage you to join the pro-activists who convert their downers into uppers.

The Free Throws

I remember when the UCLA basketball team played Notre Dame in South Bend, Indiana. With only three seconds left in the game, Notre Dame was ahead by one point. It was the crucial game of the season and the place was going wild. Suddenly a UCLA player was fouled.

His foul shots could win the game for UCLA and the Notre Dame fans roared with rage. Behind the backboard, people started waving signs and clothing, jumping up and down, and screaming.

In spite of all the distraction, the UCLA player calmly stepped up to the line and sank the first shot. Tie score.

The screams became a deafening din, but to no avail. The UCLA player sank the second shot. UCLA won the game.

Afterwards the player was interviewed by a reporter. "How could you be so cool under that intense pressure of everyone screaming at you?"

"Easy," he smiled. "I just pretended that they were all cheering for me!"

He turned a downer into an upper. And so can you!

The Stranded Passenger

A friend of mine, Fred Smith, in his book *You and Your Network,* tells about being stranded in a plane at a New York airport. After boarding the plane, he was told there would be a four-hour mechanical delay. The passengers were unhappy. One man even left the plane and lashed out angrily at the gate attendant (as if she were the one who had caused the engine malfunction).

But instead of turning hostile, Smith chose to make the best of the situation. On that dead jet, Fred began working on some of the projects in his briefcase. He said later, "Those four hours probably were the most productive I spent that year."

That's being pro-active.

The "Sugarless" Brownies

While I was on a trip, Michelle baked brownies for a singing group visiting in Miami. We had made all kinds of recipes together, so she felt like a pro.

She followed the recipe step by step, but as she was removing the hot pan from the oven, she noticed the second cup of sugar still sitting on the countertop.

It didn't faze Michelle. When I came home, she said, "Mom, I've got a new recipe—I call it 'Sugarless' Brownies. They're dietetic and they're great!"

She was right; they were. Michelle was pro-active.

What are your downers? Instead of moaning, is there any hope for making sugarless brownies? I challenge you to do the best things in the worst times. If there ever was a time for doing the best things, it is now.

6. ACCEPT WHAT YOU CANNOT CHANGE

If there is really nothing that you can do about your problem, if it's not "convert-able," then it's not your problem, but as Fred Smith says, it's your "fact of life."

Each of us, sooner or later, will have at least *one* circumstance or "fact of life" over which we have no control. I believe God allows this in our lives. Otherwise, why would we ever turn to Him? Part of the plan is to accept the less-than-perfect and the shattered dream and come at it another way. That's the essence of coping.

Earl is a friend of mine who recently received news that he had cancer. The doctor told him he had only a brief time to live and should immediately undergo chemotherapy treatments.

Earl was devastated, but headed home to tell his wife. He took her into the living room and said gently, "Honey, I have some bad news. The doctor says I have bone cancer and will have to start chemotherapy treatments."

They both began to sob, but then he composed himself

and said, "The Lord has allowed me a long and fruitful life. I have been blessed beyond measure in many ways—a wonderful family, a personal relationship with my Lord—and I'm looking forward to the hereafter with Him.

"Remember how strict I've been with my diet all these years?" he asked, suddenly cheerful. "You know how I love ice cream, especially chocolate chip. Well, on the way home I picked up two gallons, and I thought we could start celebrating right now. Let's break out the ice cream and enjoy life *today*."

My friend's attitude was one of complete acceptance. No anger, no striking back, no doubting God. He called his lawyer and began to make final arrangements that very night.

The next morning the doctor called to say, "We have made a terrible mistake. You don't have cancer! We've just examined some x-rays of your head taken thirty years ago and those same spots were evident then. There has been no change in the x-rays since that time."

Incredible error. But even more incredible was my friend's attitude.

Victory Spirit

In our community a few months ago, a most incomprehensible event occurred. Michelle's teacher, Carol Croft, a beautiful young woman in her mid-thirties, developed a sore throat on a Monday morning. By Monday afternoon she was rushed to the hospital. By Monday night she was in a coma.

We were stunned. We hoped. We prayed. For nine days Carol lay between life and death, and then on the tenth day, she died.

Her death affected not only her students, but also thousands of people throughout the city, including the members of the church where her husband, Tim, is the pastor.

Several weeks after the funeral, I took some cookies by for her three children. It was Mother's Day weekend, and my heart ached for this sad and lonely fragmented family.

The young minister thanked me profusely. I lamely mentioned something about God meeting his needs.

With joy and enthusiasm, Tim exclaimed, "Oh, He *is* meeting our needs! Losing someone I loved as much as Carol has been the most terrible thing in my life, but I know she's with the Lord. I am such a blessed man. I've had eighteen years with this wonderful woman."

He continued without tears, "And God has left me with three precious children who have an awful lot of their mother in them. We're just doing fine!"

I left, weak in the knees. What an attitude! Here is a man prepared to meet the challenges of life.

When downers come, they may knock you down, but how long you stay on the mat is up to you. William A. Ward wrote, "Adversity causes some men to break, others to break records."

Which will you choose?

4

CLAIM

Paul Harvey tells about a reporter who asked the man on the street, "What is the biggest problem in America today, ignorance or apathy?"

The man replied, "I don't know, and I don't care."

When I married Charlie, I cared desperately, but there was so much I didn't know. I had no role model for marriage as a little girl growing up. My mother was continually in the throes of divorce. All our neighbors fought like cats and dogs, and I don't remember seeing one happy marriage.

But I had a dream that someday my marriage would be the best that the world had ever seen. And when I met Charlie, I just knew that my dreams would come true. He had all the qualities I was looking for in a husband. We never had an argument. We never had a communication barrier. Everything was perfect.

And then, we got married!

In spite of my background, I felt prepared for marriage. After all, I had seen all the romantic movies, where the hero sweeps his lover off her feet, and I expected Charlie and me to ride off into the sunset the same way.

But after a few months of marriage, I was deeply disappointed. When Charlie came home at night, he didn't take me in his arms and smother me with kisses like Robert Redford did (in the movies!). Instead, he brushed right past me and went straight to the TV. My talkative, romantic husband changed. He turned into a silent, preoccupied stranger who hid behind the newspaper.

Meanwhile back at the sink drooped yours truly, Mrs. Naive Newlywed. I had assumed that we would live happily ever after, naturally. After all, love conquers all.

Who said that? Around our house, love didn't even conquer *most*.

I didn't know that conflict was inevitable. But I soon discovered that when two people are living together, conflict appears at every turn in the road. You have two different opinions on every subject—what color car to buy, where to go on vacation, how to raise the kids, or where to put the Christmas tree!

And then I had another problem—keeping organized. Perhaps you are The Organization Woman, but not this kid. I was drowning in debris.

Phyllis Diller, in telling about her disorganized housekeeping, explained, "I'm eighteen years behind in my ironing!" Then she added, "But there's no point doing it now, because it doesn't fit anybody I know."

I knew exactly how Phyllis felt. My life of moonlight and roses had changed to daylight and dishes! I only wanted to escape every afternoon with my box of bonbons to "General Hospital."

In Search of Sanity

I once read a magazine article that announced,

> *Salute to the Housewife*—Director of Transportation, Romance, Recreation, Psychology, Cuisine, Interior Design, Medicine, Horticulture, Economics, Pediatrics, Geriatrics, Direct Mail, Law, Entertainment, Religion, and Management.

What am I? A machine? A super mom? Sure, I can handle it, provided I'm fifty people at the same time.

Anyone who takes this job seriously realizes that it's difficult to become an expert in even *some* of the more basic areas, let alone all of them.

Where did we get the impression that a housewife is an expert on everything? Take kids for instance. Every young mother is supposed to be an expert on raising kids, even though she has never had any before. In fact she was just a kid herself not long ago.

For me, changing gears from the relatively carefree routine of single working woman to the tedious, monotonous, and daily routine of housewife and mother was traumatic. I felt trapped. There was no escape. Every morning it was the same old story—the dirty dishes, the unmade beds, the messy house—all closing in, suffocating, and cutting off any possibility of doing anything exciting.

Our Creator made us women very creative, with minds bursting with new ideas. Frustration comes when we cannot accomplish everything we want within a twenty-four-hour period. And if a little ankle-biter is underfoot, we often feel as if our creative days are over.

I tried to comfort myself with the thought that every human being has a similar ritual each morning, yet I saw many still accomplishing lofty goals in spite of the daily wear and tear.

As a young wife, I was on new turf and I needed help. I tried to become an expert. I looked for cram courses. I was widely read, but not thoroughly read in anything. I felt frustrated and displaced. Life was passing me by. I needed lots of answers, fast.

Instruction Manual

I called a friend and explained my problem. "You sound like the person Javan describes in his poetry," she said. Two of his thoughts did seem to describe my plight.

> I'm just a man,
>   Much like any other,
> Playing a game
>   Which is strictly ad-lib
>   Not even sure of the rules
> Going somewhere
>   Without knowing where. . . .

$$* \quad * \quad *$$

> It starts
>   At a time called birth,
> And continues

Till a time called death.
It is called Life.
It comes with no guarantees
    'Of 60 years or 60,000 miles,
        Whichever comes first.'
And somehow
    They've even left the instructions out. . . .

That can't be, I thought. *There must be instructions!* The importance of instructions came to mind again one Christmas when we gave little Laura her first tricycle. We had bought it on sale and the price did not include assembly, which didn't seem to be a problem at the time.

On that Christmas morning, sitting in the midst of discarded wrapping paper and boxes, Charlie grabbed a frame and started bolting wheels to it. He had almost finished, when in dismay he discovered a few leftover pieces.

Some wasted time and a few cross words later, he finally turned to the manual. Within a few minutes, the tricycle was finished and Laura was riding through the house dragging Christmas ribbons behind her.

Why do we insist on trial and error when the instructions are available? In the game of life, I've discovered that ignoring the Manual provided by the Inventor is like trying to build a computer from a random box of bolts and microchips. And worse than the time lost, we may mess up the whole thing by fiddling with it.

Recently I was reminded of the trouble we can get into by taking matters into our own hands. I had taken an alarm clock for repair when I noticed on the wall behind the aged clock maker, this sign:

```
┌─────────────────────────────────────────────┐
│             LABOR RATES                       │
│                                               │
│  Normal                    $12.50 per hour    │
│                                               │
│  If you wait                15.00 per hour    │
│                                               │
│  If you watch               20.00 per hour    │
│                                               │
│  If you help                30.00 per hour    │
│                                               │
│  If you laugh               40.00 per hour    │
│                                               │
│  If you worked on it first  70.00 per hour    │
│                                               │
└─────────────────────────────────────────────┘
```

Prepared by the Inventor of life, the Bible is our instruction and service manual. It is the guidebook on how to live in an unfair world. And it comes with the guarantee that those who follow it will have success in life.

Eagerly I turned to that Book. Although covered with dust, I knew that it had stood the test through the years. I flipped to Proverbs, the Book of Wisdom, written by King Solomon, the wisest man who ever lived.

I was fascinated by Solomon. I wanted his wisdom. "Read this book," he said, "and you'll find wisdom." This man had answers. Maybe not *all* the answers, but at least the right questions, and that's a start. So I began to read and ask some questions myself. Who was Solomon and how did he become so wise?

Key to Wisdom

What made this young king so special, so bright? What kind of bio did he have?

To begin with, he came from a large family. He was one of twenty children—nineteen boys and one lone miss. That's enough for a complete baseball game with two teams, one water boy, and one cheerleader.

Solomon had a beautiful mother, who could have easily been Miss Israel. His father, King of Israel, circa 1000 B.C., had first seen her when she was sunbathing in the alto-gether.

So Solomon was a palace baby. No street fights for this kid. He never knew hunger or poverty or loneliness.

Within a few short years, he was chosen to succeed his dad as king of several million Jews—a tremendous responsibility.

On Coronation Day, Solomon's first official function as King was an all-day worship service. He called the people together to praise God—military leaders, political muckety-mucks, religious big-wigs, and the cabinet.

Late that night, after the ceremonies were over, the Lord God spoke to Solomon and asked, "What one thing do you want? Ask and I'll give it to you."

Like Aladdin and the Genie with the Magic Lamp, Solomon had the opportunity to have one wish come true—an unprecedented opportunity.

What would you have asked for? Nine out of ten of us would probably have said either money or popularity or fame. If the top one hundred answers were listed for a poll, I doubt if wisdom would even have appeared. But this young man, this Rookie King, chose wisdom.

What was it that motivated Solomon to select wisdom?

First of all, he realized he desperately needed a dose of wisdom in a hurry. No time to take a four-year sabbatical to attend the University of Jerusalem on "Kings of Israel" (which class had only two previous graduates). Not even a correspondence course on Israeli history. He needed a cram course now. Right now!

Second, he realized that man's wisdom just wouldn't wash, including that of his own father, David. He had seen enough of his dad's reign to know the limits of human reasoning. Often the "wise men of Jerusalem" had recommended projects that were doomed at the outset and didn't live up to expectations. Solomon was already wise beyond his years, but he felt he needed more.

How did the Lord respond to Solomon's choice for wisdom? To say that He was pleased was the understatement of the year. The Lord gave Solomon his wish for wisdom. But He also gave him some bonus gifts, like green stamps—riches, fame, and honor like the world had never seen. He gave Solomon all the gifts that most people selfishly would have asked for in the first place.

King Solomon was consumed by the subject of wisdom. In the book of Proverbs, he mentions the word *wisdom* or *wise* 138 times in thirty-one chapters. He wrote "Learn to be wise . . . and develop good judgment and common sense! I cannot overemphasize this point. Cling to wisdom—she will protect you. Love her—she will guard you." Getting wisdom is *the most important thing you can do.*

I continued to read Solomon's proverbs, and what I discovered clobbered me. I kept coming across proverbs like, "A woman tears down her house with her own hands," (and mouth!) or "Living with a nagging woman is a continuous dripping." (Must be like a Chinese water torture!)

Those words of wisdom did a number on my attitude. I

began to see that my mental attitude often sets the environment for either uppers or downers.

Over and over I read, "Trust in the Lord with all your heart," and as I began to try, He began to change my life.

The more I read the Scriptures, the more I came to realize, as Solomon did, wisdom is available for the asking. All we need to do is claim it.

On the playground one day, a classmate asked Michelle, "How come you're so smart, Michelle? I mean, I study really hard, but you always beat me." (Ah, the blunt candor of innocent seventh graders!)

Michelle was taken aback, but she answered as honestly as she knew how, "Oh, I'm not so smart. I study hard, too, but my Mom and Dad told me that if I read the Bible every day, God promises to give me wisdom."

Michelle's friend was wide-eyed. "Really? Wow! I'm going to start reading the Bible, too!" Nothing could have pleased Michelle more.

Who encourages young people to read the Bible today? Schools certainly don't. Often the Bible is ridiculed as outdated. Many churches bypass Scripture reading. So how is this new generation going to know that the answers to life's deepest longings lie on those pages of infinite wisdom?

That's where we mothers come in. If we claim this wisdom for ourselves, then we can influence our children to do the same.

Wisdom Warehouse

When I awoke yesterday, my stomach was churning. I was chompin' at the bit to get moving. My plan for the day had thirteen major items. I knew there was no way I could accomplish everything, but I was determined to try.

First on my list was to open my Bible and take in wisdom for the day, *before* I was sinking under the load. Then I could expect God's blessing and guidance, and best of all, His wonderful presence.

As I sat in my cozy corner to read the Bible, four interruptions occurred almost simultaneously. "I might as well forget it," I sighed. But then I said to myself, "No! Even with the downers, this is your priority. Now stay with it!"

This discussion with myself occurs nearly every day. Always there are interruptions. But I know from experience that my day's schedule will lie in ruin and I'll be a basketcase by noon if I don't attend to spiritual business first.

So to start with, I read a chapter of Scripture and consider how to apply it to my life. I also try to read a chapter of Solomon's Proverbs. With thirty-one chapters in the book, there is one for each day of the month.

I am amazed at the transformation that takes place within me. I am at peace with myself. But much more than that, I have drawn near to God, He has drawn near to me, and I am fortified in my spirit to deal with the downers that are sure to come.

If your schedule is so jammed that you don't have time for one other activity, may I offer a suggestion—*listen* to Scripture instead of reading it. How? Through cassettes.

The Living Bible Paraphrased (from which I quote in this book) has produced a marvelous set of tapes. We have the entire New Testament on fourteen cassettes. All dialogue is recorded with different voices—male, female, and children. Appropriate background music makes the passages come to life. Even sound effects like crowd noises, shouting, crickets in the garden, and a rooster crowing transport you to the spot.

The nicest thing about these tapes is that you can listen during your *wasted* hours while cleaning, driving, cooking, waiting around, or taking a bath. I recently heard the entire New Testament in just one month, using only my otherwise wasted time!

First-Aid Kit

If you are in the pits today with a heavy-duty downer, you may need some first aid immediately. If so, here are some quickie samples from The Book:

> We are pressed on every side by troubles,
>   but not crushed and broken.
> We are perplexed because we don't know
>   why things happen as they do,
>   but we don't give up and quit.
> We are hunted down,
>   but God never abandons us.
> We get knocked down,
>   but we get up again and keep going.
>   2 Corinthians 4:8–9

> For I know the plans I have for you,
>   says the Lord.
> They are plans for good
>   and not for evil,
> To give you a future and a hope.
>   Jeremiah 29:11

Claim His wisdom for yourself. It is available. If this is a new activity for you, the news that "Mom reads the Bible!" will race through the family like wildfire. You will shine like a beacon in the darkness as they see God's wisdom in your life. And your family and friends will be drawn to that light.

2

Hoping for Uppers

Four Stretching Exercises to Extend Your Reach

1. Dream
2. Dare
3. Do
4. Determine

Four Stretching Exercises
to Extend Your Reach

Fort Lauderdale at Easter. One Saturday morning a group of us headed thirty miles south to Miami. I was a small-town girl from Ohio, and this was my first trip to Florida. I was about to join the thousands of college students who annually hit the beach instead of the books—spring break, Florida-style.

When we drove over the causeway from Miami to Miami Beach, passing over the Intra Coastal Waterway lined with yachts, I was lost in wonder. The sunshine sparkled like diamonds on the aqua blue bay. The strip of white beach-front hotels glistened like a Greek island nestled in the Aegean Sea.

Today, as a Miami resident, I drive that same road to Miami Beach several times a week and the scene never loses its splendor.

One afternoon a few months ago, as the skies were clearing from a furious, rain-pounding thunderstorm, I drove over the bridge just as a rainbow had formed right above the highway. The colors became more vivid with each moment, gleaming and shimmering in the moist atmosphere.

Behind me I could see in the rearview mirror dark purple clouds of the fading storm. Before me in the watercolor sky was the arch of color, the promise of God, a token of heaven for my human eyes to see. My soul was leaping inside.

This was no earthly manifestation—it was a glimpse of the world beyond. How do I know? Because God's Scriptures, in describing His throne and dwelling place, reveal the rainbow as one of the decorations.

The rainbow is the closest glimpse of heaven we have on earth. The God who flung the universe into being and braided the rings around Saturn, displays a touch of His glory in the rainbow.

Imagine! He takes a multicolor beam, bends it with His hands, and hangs it in the sky to grace our world for a few moments. The Great Master Painter from the faraway hills is doing a number in the sky.

How many even notice? I wanted to honk at the drivers in the cars passing by and point to the glory. Surely, they must see it! But as I glanced at the car next to mine, I saw the driver's stone face staring straight ahead. How could he be oblivious to such beauty?

"Concentrate on the road, Marabel," I told myself. "Don't get carried away. Maybe not everyone notices. You can't do anything about that, but make sure you notice. Tell Charlie and the girls tonight. Thank the Lord."

As I viewed the panorama from the top of the bridge, I thought, this is like the Bridge to Tomorrow. Forget the stormclouds behind, look only to the sun and rainbow ahead.

Behind Every Cloud

In the introduction to "Coping with Downers," the question was asked, "Is it possible to make it through today without any downers?"

We found out that downers are inevitable. That's a given. But the challenge lies in how you will respond when trouble hits. You can approach each downer as an opportunity for turning it into an upper. How exciting!

And what about uppers? Can we count on them? Unfortunately not. Uppers aren't guaranteed, remember?

One of my friends was offended by that premise. "How can you say such a thing?" she demanded. "My dear, life is full of uppers! I'm an upper person. Why, just the fact that the sun comes up and you're breathing is an upper!"

"I agree wholeheartedly," I replied. "If you see it, it's an upper. But there is no guarantee you'll be here to see the sun come up tomorrow."

Not long ago, when a weather report in the evening newspaper omitted a word, the forecast read,

---

WEATHER FORECAST

50 percent chance of tonight or tomorrow

A mistake of course, but true nonetheless. There are no guarantees of tomorrow.

Several years ago, news reporter Margarite Higgins interviewed soldiers fighting on the 38th Parallel in Korea. One tired and discouraged young soldier had been on the front line for weeks, never knowing when or if the mortar shells would take their toll. "Soldier," she asked, "if I could give you one thing, what would it be?"

"Give me tomorrow!" he cried.

No one can guarantee you tomorrow. But I can encourage you to make the most of today.

Cramming for Finals

I once saw a cartoon of a father telling his young son, "In this game of life, there are no 'time-outs.' The clock is always ticking." If you are like most people I know, there are not enough hours in the day, so we haven't a minute to lose!

Do you know how to accomplish *twice* as much today as you planned? Pretend you're going on vacation in the morning. You would really make tracks today if you were leaving at 6:00 A.M. tomorrow.

Over the entrance hall at Harvard University is the quote by Henry David Thoreau: "Students should not play at life or study it merely, while the community supports them at this expensive game. They should earnestly live life from beginning to end. Me thinks this would exercise their minds as much as mathematics."

Earnestly live life from beginning to end! With such an attitude, uppers are certainly more likely to happen.

One New Year's Day, pastor Browning Ware of Austin, Texas, told his congregation, "I hope your purpose for living this year is larger than you are."

What a great resolution. I hope your purpose for living today is larger than you are.

You will never know your potential until you stretch. Here are four stretching exercises to help you extend your reach.

5

DREAM

My friend Andrea looked down at her iced mocha drink while trying to drown her gloom and said, "I really don't know what's the matter with me. David and I are doing fine, the kids are fine, everything's fine. But I've lost all my motivation. Really. I just don't care about anything."

I nodded in compassion. I have been there, too. Most people hit a low plateau occasionally, and for its duration, they feel despair—like they won't pull out of it.

Psychologists have all sorts of theories for this malady. I suspect it's partly due to the intense pressure that modern man imposes on himself. We want the best. We want to be the best. We push and shove to get ahead and sometimes we just plain short out. The body and the emotions cry out, "Enough, already!"

My friend Andrea wanted to start her engine again, but couldn't seem to flick the switch.

Suddenly I had an idea. Perhaps she could glimpse life from another perspective. "Listen," I said, "I want to try an experiment. Tell me the things that you are most proud of in your life. All your greatest accomplishments. Imagine that you have only forty-eight hours to live. If you were ready to wrap it up, what would you want to include in your obituary?"

Andrea looked startled and laughed nervously.

"Seriously," I encouraged. "Write down your accomplishments."

She began to write on her napkin, "Graduated from Ohio State with honors, married wonderful man, three beautiful children, Chairman of the Cancer Auxiliary . . ."

"OK, Andrea, good. Now do you have any regrets? Is there anything you wish you had done that you didn't?"

"Well, of course," she said, "don't you?"

She wrote a few items on the other side of her napkin.

"Now," I said, "I have an assignment for you. No doubt you have much more than forty-eight hours left. For the moment, forget about your accomplishments and look at your regrets instead. Why not set these as goals to be accomplished? Why not start to work on the entire list?"

She raised her eyebrows and shrugged as if to say, "Why not?"

Suddenly she looked at her watch. "I'm late for the kids, I've got to go. Thanks so much for lunch." She ran out clutching her napkin. She was on her way.

Fred Smith once told me, "One should plan life while sitting on a tombstone." From that vantage point, Andrea had gained a new perspective.

During the Christmas season, our church choir performed at a psychiatric ward. As we entered the doors of the meeting room, elderly patients leaning against the walls and sitting in wheelchairs stared curiously as though something were wrong with all of *us*.

The program began. I glanced at a large sign on the wall. Composed with red interchangeable letters, it contained the following information:

> The year is 1985.
> Yesterday was SATURDAY.
> Today is SUNDAY.
> Tomorrow is MONDAY.
> The weather outside is WARM.
> The president is RONALD REAGAN.

This billboard included all of the news that was necessary for these patients. It represented their entire newspaper. But the more I thought about it, I realized that some of my acquaintances who are not in institutions exist on just such limited information. All they care about is the day of the week, whether it's going to rain, and if the President is still in charge.

Watchman Nee wrote, "When we lose the tension between where we are and where we ought to be, we plateau." But I believe, when we fail to dream bigger than where we are, we don't even plateau, we slide back.

I agree with what Henry Ford said, "A poor man is not that one without a cent; a poor man is that one without a dream."

Don't be caught dead without a dream. You can turn your "I wish I had" into "I think I can" by creating the environment, imagining the possibility, and picturing the reality. Here are some tips on how to do it.

1. CREATE THE ENVIRONMENT

At a holiday party, Charlie and I were introduced to a guest who had just returned from a five-week trip through Europe. I asked him if he had taken any pictures. "Nope," he said. "Didn't see nuthin' to take pictures of."

I stared at this old codger in disbelief. Incredible! The world so filled with wonder, and he had missed it.

I couldn't help but think of that Saturday morning when I first gave Michelle a camera and turned her loose. I was amazed at her results—pictures of a butterfly on a branch, a cat asleep under a bush, a flower in bloom, and a plane ten miles overhead. Through the eyes of a child, creativity is rampant.

One summer morning, when she was nine, Michelle climbed out on a tree limb overhanging the garage. From this high perch, she began writing *The Diary of a Cat*. Her cat, Sneakers, had curled up in a ball at the base of the tree, to the great irritation of the German shepherd next door.

Now it's hard for me to imagine a four-legged viewpoint of life from six inches off the ground, but to Michelle it was easy as pie. Look over her shoulder and read her cat diary.

"I thought to myself, *Those dogs. What beasts! Those bushy-tailed, long-eared beasts! And their language! (Hey Butch, wanna come over to my pad tonight and play poker with the guys?) Aren't those animals despicable?*

"*I am a cat—a sensible, beautiful cat. Cats have a very unique language: 'Meow, Meow, Meow, Meow.' We are truly a gorgeous*

group of animals! I am happy to say that I can't say much about those, those dogs! Barking, jumping up on people, waking up the neighbors!

"(STOP WRITING IN DIARY. STAND UP AND STRETCH.) Well, I've written in my diary enough today. (CURL UP ON SOFA OR BED, START MEOWING SOFTLY—GO TO SLEEP.)"

You may not want to climb a tree over your garage, but in order to set the environment for creativity, it helps to be alone, free from all distractions.

Get-Away Hide-Away

Where is your get-away? In the library stacks? Or in your car parked by the side of the road? Or in a pastoral park? Or in a corner within your own four walls? It doesn't matter where, just as long as you're safe from the television and telephone. Give your creativity a chance to bloom, and when it does, don't lose it.

Sir Francis Bacon years ago suggested carrying a pencil at all times. "A man would do well to carry a pencil in his pocket and write down the thought of the moment. Those that come unsought are commonly the most valuable and should be secured, because they seldom return."

Many of my creative insights are born in the shower or in the car or in bed late at night, and unless I write them down, I seldom recall them. It helps, I've found, to have a note pad by the bed, in the car, and in the bathroom.

One of the world's great orchestral conductors, Riccardo Muti (music director of the Philadelphia Symphony Orchestra, conductor laureate of the Philharmonia Orchestra of London, and soon-to-be music director of La Scala in Milan), has another approach to creating a stretching environment.

In an interview for *Vogue* magazine (Sept. 1984), appropriately entitled "Conducting Electricity," conductor Muti was asked how he approaches a new musical composition.

He explained his secret, "When I decide I will study a score, I start by having it on my piano, even if I don't turn the first page for months. It is like an old-fashioned courtship. I like to know it's there; I feel warmer and warmer toward it, then, when I feel really ready, I turn the first page. I study, analyze, live without it for a certain period, then, after two months, I go back to it again."

What is the environment that enables you to be your most creative? As an exercise to start the rusty wheels turning again, let your mind travel back to your childhood and try looking at life through the eyes of a child.

2. IMAGINE THE POSSIBILITY

The full-page ad by Boeing Aircraft was entitled, "Tomorrow You Can Be Anywhere." The ad was gripping in its call.

"TOMORROW you could be having a candlelight dinner, just the two of you, a thousand miles away from business phones and your 6:00 A.M. alarm clock.

"TOMORROW you could be stretched out on the warm sand reading a good whodunit.

"TOMORROW you could be walking the fairway of a championship course.

"TOMORROW you could be snorkeling in the clearest, bluest water in all the world.

"TOMORROW you could be climbing castles.

"TOMORROW you could be volleying with the club pro on a court you've seen a hundred times on TV.

"TOMORROW you could be headed back to your stomping grounds with your family.

"TOMORROW you could be strapped into a harness fighting to reel in what looks like the biggest fish you've ever seen.

"TOMORROW you could say to yourself 'I am running away from home. If I don't do it now, I probably never will. No ifs, ands, or buts about it. No putting it off any more. Good-bye pounding pavement. Hello soft, warming sand.'

"Go. Now. Before all those precious tomorrows turn into never."

Boeing has a great idea, but I'll tell you how you can travel even farther, and at far less cost, without a 747.

Take a mind trip, and let yourself dream. It works.

"Imagination is as good as many voyages," said George William Curtis, "and much cheaper!"

The genius Albert Einstein once reflected, "When I examined myself and my methods of thought, I came to the conclusion that the gift of fantasy has meant more to me than my talent for absorbing positive knowledge. . . . Imagination is more important than knowledge."

Dream Cruiser

As a child, I loved to read to escape reality. I could instantly transport myself to faraway places. Since we didn't own a car and never took a vacation, that was my only form of travel.

As a teenager, I spent many afternoons lying in the leaf-covered woods near our house, looking up through the tree boughs, dreaming. It was there that I planned my someday trip to Europe.

116

When I told my mother my plans, she laughed. For a poor little kid in Ohio, going to Europe was a virtual impossibility. My mother couldn't help but laugh, and I was crushed. But that laugh did wonders for me. Europe became my goal, my passion.

My next problem was money. We had none. So I went back to the woods to dream. I pictured myself dipping soup in the galley of a ship en route to Europe, but I ended up cutting hair in the hometown salon. I finally saved enough to sail as a paying tourist aboard the *Queen Elizabeth.* The reality was beyond my wildest dreams!

What are *you* dreaming? If your mind can conceive it, it's a possible dream. No major goal starts without a dream.

As Bloody Mary in *South Pacific* asked the Stingy Stinker from Philadelphia, "If you don't have a dream, how you gonna make your dream come true?"

Free-Wheeling

Many short-range goals change from week to week, but heart-deep dreams can nestle in and grow into life goals.

Want to hear my current dream? Within the next five-year time frame, I am planning to pack up my gear, dress in khaki Alpine shorts, and speed over the French Alps on my trusty (or rusty!) bike.

When I told Charlie my goal, he laughed and said, "You'll probably only last five miles." There's that laugh again. But that's all I needed. If you're a maverick, expect static.

Charlie may be right. However, as I train in my neighborhood, I realize that whether or not I ever really make the trip through France is not the issue. The pursuit of my dream is as rewarding as the French bike ride itself will be.

Family Brainstorming

What is the most exciting day of a vacation?
(a) The day you first dream about it.
(b) The day you decide to go.
(c) The day before you leave.
(d) The day you leave.
(e) The day you return.

Last month, to find the answer, I took an informal poll among some friends. This was not a poll worthy of "ABC Nightly News," but the results were interesting nonetheless. The answer most people gave was "(a) The day you first dream about it."

If that's so—if the fun is in the dreaming—why do we

squelch our imagination when we grow up and become "mature"?

Alex Osborne's best-selling book, *Applied Imagination,* gives successful techniques for reinstilling the gift of fantasy. Osborne works mainly with business executives who live in a pragmatic, squeeze-out-the-buck, pressure cooker.

One of his techniques involves a fantasy session called "Brainstorming" in which all suggestions, no matter how ludicrous, are displayed on a blackboard. The more outrageous, the better. To encourage creativity, which is often slow to start, no critical comments are allowed during this session. The leader rings a bell if a negative comment is made. Of course, not all of the ideas culminate in great sales programs, but at least new opportunities are explored and the creative juices start flowing.

You can use this same technique with your family. Try a little brainstorming tonight. During dinner, ask for suggestions concerning the neighborhood crime problem, or Junior's future career goals, or something as simple as planning Sunday's supper. You may be surprised at the results.

And more than that, you may have stimulated some unused mental muscles—a great stretching exercise in itself. Supreme Court Justice Oliver Wendell Holmes once said, "Man's mind once stretched by a new idea, never regains its original dimensions."

3. Picture the Reality

Roger Staubach, former quarterback for the Dallas Cowboys, once accompanied Bill Glass in a prison crusade. Glass opened the meeting by asking the inmates, "When you were young, how many of you had fathers who said, 'When you grow up, you're gonna end up in jail'?" Staubach was shocked to see most of the prisoners raise their hands.

After the meeting, Jim Sundberg, then the star catcher for the Texas Rangers, said to Staubach, "Roger, do you know what my father said to me when I was growing up? Over and over he said, 'Some day when you grow up, son, you're going to be a major league catcher!'"

A parent can influence his child to be the best. Sundberg had pictured the reality of his father's words.

During the U.S. Open several years ago, Jack Nicklaus was in second place, only one stroke behind the leader, Tom Watson. But then Watson hit his next shot into the rough by the eighteenth green.

Big trouble. Golfers across America held their breath as they watched on TV.

Watson carefully studied his predicament and pitched the ball onto the green. It rolled and rolled, dead straight at the hole—and dropped in! The gallery erupted in a roar.

After the tournament, reporters asked Watson, the new U.S. Open Champion, "Did you know it was going to go in?"

"I told my caddy before I hit it, 'I'm gonna knock it into the hole,'" smiled the new champion.

What do you want out of life? Do you want it badly enough to pay the price? Have you created the necessary environment? Have you imagined the possibility? Have you pictured the reality? That picture may be a small step for mankind, but a giant step for you. Once you've taken it, you're on your way.

Note to Readers: The next chapter, *"Dare,"* is only for those with an unfulfilled dream. All others may skip to the following chapter.

6

DARE

Do you know anyone who isn't in a hurry? Most of our friends live at an unbelievably fast pace. Offices that for years relied on the mails for communication now use Telex lines, Federal Express, and courier services as a matter of course. Americans place great premium on speed, spawning the need for new businesses daily—"quick-fix-it" shops, one-hour cleaners, convenience stores, twenty-four-hour bank tellers, instant potatoes, fast-food chains, satellite communications, same day service, and passport photos while-you-wait.

When I wake up each morning, my motor is already racing. I feel like I'm behind before the day has even begun.

Yet I start each day with every good intention. I make a most ambitious checklist. But by the end of the day, I hardly ever accomplish all that I set out to do.

Take yesterday. My list was jammed with errands and appointments. By 5:00 P.M. half the list remained undone, and strains of "The Unfinished Symphony" kept time with my pounding headache.

Why am I unable to complete my list? One reason is those daily downers I don't expect.

Another reason is I don't really *intend* to accomplish all that I've written down. In fact, if I were brutally honest I could tell you in the morning what items would remain unfinished by 9 o'clock that night.

As I look over my list for today, what I see are really three different lists—(1) Those Things I Must Accomplish Today; (2) Those Things I Can Put Off Until Tomorrow; and (3) Those Things I May Do Someday.

1. *Today.* Some items are for certain. I must go to the store (we're out of milk), then to the library (two books overdue), then visit with a priest from Manila (he wrote asking to meet during a forty-minute layover between flights), and then pick up Michelle and her friend Melissa by 3:00 P.M.

None of these items is difficult, they just take time. Most simply fall in the category of errands. (Wouldn't it be wonderful if only we could anticipate a week's worth of errands, and do them all at once? But life doesn't work that way.)

I can handle the "Today" items. They are within easy reach, and I have great confidence that I will take care of them.

Mission Probable. My degree of commitment: Strong.

2. *Tomorrow.* Other items on my list for today include the things I carried over from yesterday—like taking a fruit basket to a friend in the hospital, or writing my college roommate, or hemming up Michelle's uniforms for next semester.

Even though they keep appearing on my list, deep inside I know they'll be done "tomorrow."

This list contains the tedious, the project without a deadline, the things I've lost the joy for doing. Postponing them till tomorrow seems more convenient.

There's no question that I am capable of accomplishing the "tomorrow" duties today, but I put them off because I am either confused or indecisive about them.

Mission Possible. My degree of commitment: Weak.

3. *Someday.* And then there are projects on my list that are absolutely out of reach today.

I am not dead set on doing any of these difficult or poorly pictured projects. Actually, from my perspective today, I know that I am incapable of accomplishing them.

For example, there's just no way I'll be able to finish reading that book I started last week—at least not today. And I won't be able to start those Spanish lessons either, not to mention a serious workout program.

In other words, *Mission Impossible. My degree of commitment: None.*

This last category of "Someday" obviously needs the most work. Just thinking of these items clouds my agenda and drains my energy. My first step then is either to begin work on them as actual projects or strike them completely from my life.

The next step is to arrange my projects in their order of priority so that the important ones will be accomplished.

My lawyer-husband, Charlie, has a unique system for arranging his projects. He uses five paperweights on his office desk. Each one represents a different priority.

Do When Convenient

Do Now

Urgent

By Order of Court

In Contempt

It is so easy to stay busy with the time-consuming interruptions, while the *truly important* pile remains untouched.

Successful executives try to avoid falling into this trap, but it's never easy. Why? As President Eisenhower once said, "The urgent is seldom important and the important is seldom urgent." It takes a strong will to resist the urgent.

Dallas businesswoman Mary Crowley, who went from home executive to president of Home Interiors, Inc., a company with sales over three hundred million dollars annually, shares one of her success secrets in her book, *You Can Too*.

"Worry," she writes, "never robs tomorrow of its sorrow; it only saps today of its strength. If I felt myself falling into the trap of self-pity, I learned to sit up and do something constructive immediately. If I felt tired, I gained energy by telling myself when I got up in the morning that I felt great. If I dreaded an especially worrisome task, I chose to do it first and get it out of the way."

The late Indira Gandhi also admitted that she struggled with this same problem while serving as Prime Minister of India. In a letter published by *Time* magazine, she wrote, "I am full of ideas, but I haven't the driving force and energy to execute them. One has to fight so much for every little thing. I was born bone lazy, so I have developed a system of dividing things into most important, important, less important, and I fight only for the first. Sometimes I am very fit and energetic for the second as well."

Do you find yourself putting off essential projects that you know should have high priority? Do they intimidate you?

So many times I am stopped cold by "The Can't Barrier." I tell myself, "I can't do it!" But if I break through that barrier just once, I can then move on into new frontiers.

Here are five questions I ask myself when I need help breaking "The Can't Barrier."

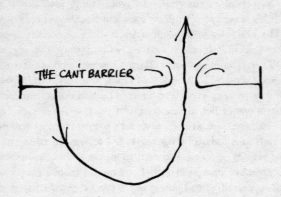

1. AM I BEING HONEST WITH MYSELF?

What prevents us from taking action in a new direction? Cop outs and excuses—every excuse under the sun. I have them. You have them. Some are founded; some are not.

Ever wonder why we are so proficient at making excuses? Maybe it's because we do it so much. We have been practicing the fine art of making excuses since we were kids.

A public school teacher once shared some notes she had received, allegedly written by parents excusing their children from school. These little gems are tributes to a special kind of creativity.

• "Dear School: Please accuse John from being absent to January 28, 29, 30, 31, 32, and also 33."

• "Please execute Bobby for being. It was his father's fault."

• "My son is under the doctor's care and should not take fiziacal ed. Please execute him."

Cute. But who's kidding whom?

Take another look at your "Someday List." Are you sincerely interested in these projects? Are you holding back because of a barrier—real or imagined? Don't con yourself. It's only yourself you're kidding.

2. DOES "I CAN'T" MEAN "I WON'T"?

Charlie and I once planned a party for some junior high school students at Christmastime. One of the girls in the youth group could play the piano (no Van Cliburn, but she wasn't bad). We asked her to play for the party and she said, "Oh, no, I can't. I'm not good enough." We pleaded and encouraged, but she refused.

Why does a person say, "I can't," when she often means, "I won't"?

One reason may be shyness, or fear of failure. Phoebe Phobia revisited. Many of us hold back and think, "I can't. I'm afraid of what might happen."

Psychologist Philip G. Zimbardo says that shyness is "an excessive concern for security and unwillingness to take a risk to challenge the system." He estimates that 40 percent of all Americans consider themselves shy. Even such notables as President Jimmy Carter, Prince Charles, Barbara Walters, and Catherine Deneuve, reputed to be the most beautiful woman in the world, suffer from this malady.

Many times a shy person will set up unreasonable standards of perfection for herself and not take action until all risks have been removed.

In Ecclesiastes, chapter 11, King Solomon defused his problems this way, "If you wait for perfect conditions, you will never get anything done."

3. AM I CAPABLE OF MORE?

Have you ever felt threatened because someone else did something better than you? I have. Often.

Now, when that happens, I ask myself whether I am capable of more. If not, why should I worry about it? If I'll never run a four-minute mile, why worry about the Olympic tryouts in June? But if I can, then that can be a positive force to motivate me onward.

I encourage my daughters to do the best that they can—that's all any of us can do. But how often do we really live up to our potential? Seeing the accomplishments of someone with more limitations than I have inspires me to try harder.

I was recently inspired by the movie, *He Leadeth Me*, the story of Ken Medema who was born blind. When Ken's parents realized there was no medical hope of restoring his sight, they determined to treat him as a normal child. As time went by, they taught him how to play games and ride a bike and water ski.

Years later, one day on campus, he bumped into another

blind college student who said, "Hey, watch it. Don't you know I'm blind?"

"Oh, I'm sorry," Ken apologized. "I didn't see you."

Ken attributes his positive outlook on life to concentrating on the things he could do, instead of the things he couldn't do. "The handicap," he says, "is not the blindness. Everyone is handicapped, some to a lesser degree than others. *A handicap*," Ken says, "*is whatever keeps you from operating at your best.* But a handicap is not bad. It may be the thing that motivates you—that really gets you going. Say to whatever paralyzes you, 'I will triumph over you. I will conquer you. You will not have dominion over me.' That may be the most exciting and spiritually rewarding thing that ever happens to a person."

Ken's father counseled him many times over the years, "Son, you can sit down and feel sorry for yourself, or you can get up and live."

And isn't that the bottom line for any of us? We can sit around and feel sorry for ourselves, or we can get up and live. What about you? Are you capable of more?

4. IS THE REWARD WORTH THE RISK?

Early one spring, we discussed plans for vacation at supper one night. Charlie told us we'd be heading for Colorado and asked for ideas.

"I don't care where we go," chimed in Laura, "as long as we can ride horses." (A stock reply from a sixteen-year-old would-be veterinarian.)

Michelle spoke up next, "I just want to stop by the side

of the road and climb mountains." (A twelve-year-old geologist speaking.)

I wanted to head to the mountains for cool weather. (In mid-July in Miami you'll find me crouched on the lower shelf of the refrigerator. So I was looking forward to some of God's homemade air-conditioning.)

Charlie wanted to travel and see Colorado like a native. We booked airline reservations to Denver and made arrangements to rent a car, but deliberately left the itinerary open, planning on a committee vote as we went along.

That was a big mistake. We soon learned Morgan's First Law of Decision-Making on Vacations: As the number of people traveling together increases, the chances for accommodating personal wishes of all (or any) of the family decreases in inverse proportion. Or said another way, the person who said you could please everyone on vacation must have had the kids locked up in a U-Haul trailer.

But the interstate highways were marvelous—constant reminders that some of our tax money went for a worthy cause. We were proud to think that we helped pay for the guard rails at the Colorado Springs interchange.

The only difference between an interstate in Colorado and other states is the scenery. Magnificent, rugged, snow-capped-in-summer mountain peaks are visible from most highways.

Near the tiny gold-mining town of Ouray, high in the Rockies, we parked by a rushing stream to hike. Michelle was halfway up a hill before Charlie had turned off the motor. I soon discovered that those beautiful snow-capped peaks on the horizon somehow puff up their chests in an act of defiance the moment someone starts to climb them.

Gingerly we climbed up through the woods until we were

out of sight and sound of the highway. We lapped from the ice-cold, crystal-clear stream. The fragrance of pine filled the crisp air. Under foot was the crunch of pine branches and needles. Nature's radio was playing a hundred different bird songs with the backup of a rushing mountain stream. What a symphony!

Meanwhile, Michelle, who had plunged on ahead, broke my reverie by shouting, "Mom, come up here. There's a waterfall!"

We all scrambled up the hill, and sure enough, within a few moments we came upon the most magnificent waterfall we'd ever seen.

We picked our way over slippery wet pebbles leading up, up, until the overspray soaked us. The roar of the falls was thunderous, and the tremendous surge of power cascading down, awesome. I wanted to freeze that moment forever. We had ventured and it had paid off in a memory we'd never forget.

That night, back at the motel, we relived our adventure. The trek in the woods, though only a day, would last forever in our hearts. We compared interstate highways with inner woods. I never dreamed that my city-living family would prefer the discomfort of the woods to the comfort of the highway. But they never once complained of blisters and poison ivy and rock slides.

MAIN HIGHWAY	NEW TRAIL
Comfortable	Uncomfortable
Safe	Risky
Predictable	Unpredictable
Well Defined	Uncertain
Well Traveled	Uncharted
Relaxing	On Edge
Boring	Exciting

What are the risks involved in your project? Do these include possible embarrassment or failure? Fear of the unknown, the unproven, the untested?

Shooting rapids, scaling mountains, and taming lions certainly conjure up pictures of risk. But so does grinding it out in a dog-eat-dog world, be that in a career, a marriage, or a family. Life itself is a moment-by-moment risk.

5. AM I WILLING TO START?

"To begin is half the work," wrote a fourth-century Roman poet named Decimus Magnus Ausonius. And according to a Chinese proverb, if you deliberate fully before taking a step, you may spend your entire life on one leg.

Risking means taking the first step. Consider the following individuals who, in spite of circumstances, overcame "The Can't Barrier." They rejected the typical excuses.

What is your excuse? Could it be one of the following?

• *"But I'm too old."*

So was baseball pitcher Satchel Paige, who asked, "How old would you be if you didn't know how old you was?" Age is a state of mind.

• *"But I'm too small."*

So is Tim Howard, a short football linebacker from Texas, who says, "I think my size is my greatest asset; people always write me off."

• *"But I'm not good enough yet."*

Winston Churchill summed up the problem well when he said, "The maxim that nothing matters but perfection is spelled P-A-R-A-L-Y-S-I-S."

• *"But I'm too handicapped."*

So was Helen Keller, who proclaimed, "I thank God for my handicaps, for through them I have found myself, my work, and my God."

Are you capable of more? Are you willing to start? The first question depends on ability; the second on desire. Lack of ability is sometimes overcome by intense desire. But ability without desire will hardly ever develop full potential.

If you are ready to start, as a symbol of your new resolve, and to gear up your momentum, turn over your mattress today (but not with Fred on it!).

If you dream of finishing your college education, or applying to law school, or learning French, or changing careers—start now. And don't be discouraged when the first downer hits. It may take a fine balancing act to handle your daily tasks of school or marriage or career.

I have found encouragement for my own balancing act from a plaque hanging in the lobby of my doctor's office. The words are by Jacob Furth.

> With one hand we seek to maintain a thoughtful, orderly . . . predictable line of investigation sustaining productivity from one day to the next, while with the other we reach for the stars.

Mark Twain also had some encouraging words when he said, "The man with a new idea is a crank, until the idea succeeds."

Congratulations to you former "cranks" who have made it! And to all you would-be stars on the horizon, your day will come.

DO

When Laura headed off to Wheaton College in late August, our whole family made a mini-vacation out of the trip to Chicago.

I was concerned how I would fare when it came time to say good-bye, so I asked a friend how she handled it when her son went to football camp before college classes started.

"We held each other while I cried," she told me.

And then her huge linebacker son cleared his throat and said, "I know how you feel, Mom. I'd cry, too, if I weren't so cool."

Her story didn't particularly comfort me, but I knew I'd get through it somehow. Actually, when the moment came, I wept delicately. Laura was grinning at all the freshmen milling around the sidewalk and seemed rather eager to have us wrap it up. "I love you, Mom," she told me, "but I just don't feel like crying."

As our car pulled away, she was already absorbed into a group of excited students, and that scene helped dry the ocean in my heart.

We headed back to Miami, driving 640 miles the first day. Finally, we pulled into a motel in Louisville, and I ran into the room to call Laura. I wanted to make sure she had survived the first day at college alone (without me!).

Her words rang through the phone, "Mom! I'm in love!"

Charlie got on the telephone and asked dryly, "Laura, what took you so long?"

Since then Laura calls every time a new love comes on the scene (our phone bills are enormous!). Charlie worries that her studies seem less important than the guys, and occasionally reminds her to leave a little room for classes in her busy social schedule.

Self-discipline and dedication to study usually come only after years of schooling, but in the meantime, tests and grades are often the only coercion to keep students motivated.

Looking back on my own school years, I can now see the advantage of a report card to help keep score. It held me accountable and gave me an objective standard against which to measure my performance—not only in comparison with my peers, but with myself as well.

If I were given a report card currently for Accomplishment and Effort and Conduct in life, I am not sure I would like it, but I would want only one grade to appear, and that is A+, excellence in all areas.

Here are my four self-imposed requirements for excellence.

1. EXCELLENCE REQUIRES A SELF-IMPOSED SEPARATION

I have recently taken up the game of golf, but it's rough. I am still trying to learn how to hit the ball. I don't even know how to hold the caddie!

Charlie has encouraged me to read all sorts of golf magazines. They don't turn me on like they do Charlie, but I was impressed by several professional golfers' comments.

Ray Floyd says, "It's a lot easier to be a mediocre player than a good player. Life is easier, demands on your time are less, you don't have to practice as much, you don't have to have the dedication. But once you decide that you want to be a good player, not an also-ran, you've made your decision and that's dedication."

Whole-hearted dedication is self-imposed separation. The time involved in perfecting skills will naturally separate you from other activities.

When it comes to golf, I am not willing to sacrifice other activities for the game, but I will take that principle and apply it somewhere else.

Excellence separates. The excellent performance stands out from the average in any area—in the kitchen, the athletic field, the office, or the classroom.

2. Excellence Requires a Self-Imposed Sacrifice

Warren Wiersbe asks in his book, *The High Cost of Shortcuts*, "What are you cutting short?" If you are saving time and energy in the kitchen or classroom or the office, that's a help. Shortcuts help make life run smoothly. But sacrifice, not shortcuts, is required over the long haul for excellence. It's called paying the price, denying momentary pleasures for a further gain.

Another golfing great, Jack Nicklaus, when asked about his motivation in the game of golf, replied, "How often you win or lose . . . depends almost entirely on how effectively you learn to manage the game's two ultimate adversaries: the course and yourself. Managing *the course* takes patience," says Nicklaus. "Managing *yourself* requires intelligence and emotional control. Both, like learning to hit the shots, require perseverance."

Take it from the champ. Excellence requires sacrifice, not the quick fix.

3. EXCELLENCE REQUIRES A SELF-IMPOSED STANDARD

When the late famed Mies van der Rohe taught architecture, he required his students to draw in every single brick in an entire wall. He said, "It will force the stonemasons to put in the precise number of bricks. Only then can you be sure that the fine detailing at the edges will come out the way you want them to come out."

Van der Rohe's philosophy and motivation for excellence came from Scripture. Over and over he reiterated, "God is in the details." Attention to the details—that little touch made the difference between thousands of architects and one special architect.

GOD IS IN THE DETAILS

Don Shula, the super coach of the Miami Dolphins, also knows the importance of details. Reacting to a player's mistake in practice, Coach Shula said, "We never let an error go unchallenged. Uncorrected errors will multiply. Someone once asked me if there wasn't benefit in overlooking one small flaw. I asked him, 'What *is* a small flaw?'"

Success lies in the details. Set your standard high. Actively avoid mediocrity. You will increase opportunities for uppers and add insulation against downers. You may not end up Number One, but you'll sleep well at night knowing that you gave it your very best.

4. EXCELLENCE REQUIRES A SELF-IMPOSED SPECIALIZATION

A young man stopped by a construction site to see his friend, Tom. He was told, "Tom doesn't work here anymore."

The young man himself was looking for work, so he asked, "Has the vacancy been filled?"

The supervisor replied, "Tom didn't leave no vacancy."

What an indictment to one's very being! If I thought my husband or my children or my boss or my God would say the same thing, I'd pack it in right now.

We live in a world of specialization. To achieve excellence, we must narrow the focus of our time and energy and concentrate on the area for which we are each best suited. Diversity is what keeps the world moving.

What is your specialty? Find your niche, and then work to become the very best. Give it all you have.

Someone once said that the one who performs with excellence is like a duck—smooth and unruffled on top, but paddling like mad underneath.

Excellence requires self-imposed separation, sacrifice, standard, and specialization. Self-imposed? That simply means no one else can do it for you.

Every job is a self-portrait of the person who does it. Autograph your work with excellence.

8

DETERMINE

First noticed her when I started the car that summer morning. She was climbing frantically. Up and up she went until she finally reached her goal and stopped on top of the car aerial. This bug was some kind of lady. A ladybug, as a matter of fact. I gave her a mental cheer and backed out of the driveway.

At the stop light I glanced over and there she was, still hanging on to the aerial for dear life. A slight drizzle started and I turned on my wipers. But no problem for Lady. She was an all-weather climber.

As I drove, I thought about the endurance of my little friend. Comparing bug size to my size, Lady's performance would be like my climbing a flagpole ninety feet high in one minute during hurricane force winds and rain!

What an incredible creature, this little bug. I was exhausted just thinking of her adventure.

At the next light, she turned and headed downward, even faster than she had made the trip going up.

Out of respect I waited until she was back on Terra Fender before I moved. Honking horns notwithstanding, I felt better just knowing she had made it safely.

As you leave for work tomorrow or walk across the sidewalk, watch out for Lady. She's tough and determined, but she might not survive a direct hit.

Lady's persistence was a living example to me. She probably thought she was a goner, but she hung in there and made it.

How Much Longer?

Persistence is the twin sister of excellence. One is a matter of quality; the other a matter of time. One concerns detail; the other, duration.

A friend once sent me a card with the message,

Nothing can take the place of persistence—
> *Talent will not:*   Nothing is more common than
> unsuccessful men with talent.
>
> *Genius will not:*   Unrewarded genius is almost a
> proverb.
>
> *Education will not:* The world is full of educated
> derelicts.

During the past few years a lot of women have written me asking for advice on their own marriage. I am not a counselor, and there's no magic potion I can prescribe for their problems. Yet nevertheless, the letters come—long, handwritten, many-paged letters that sometimes leave me in

141

tears. I wish I could answer each one individually and follow-up with a personal visit. But, of course, that's impossible.

One of the most typical questions came from a lady in Houston who wrote, "I have read your book. I have tried your principles for the last few weeks, but so far there has been no response from Tom. How long do I have to keep this up?"

Who am I to say whether her marriage or any other is capable of resurrection? But whether it's hanging by a thread or a rope, I believe if there's life, there's hope.

I have seen some of the most incredible turnarounds in what seemed to be terminal marriages. I remember one New York fashion model whose husband abused her physically and emotionally. For two years she was beaten and cursed. Still she stayed. I'll never know why, except she said she loved him.

She told me over lunch one day, "I'm going to make this marriage work if it kills me."

I said, "It will. This is insane! Get out while you can," but she stayed.

We lost touch with each other. Three years later we met again. She was so excited she grabbed me and started telling me about her wonderful marriage.

"Are you remarried?" I asked.

"Oh, no, it's George. I'm so glad I hung in there then."

Today he is a changed man because of what she did. They are a walking miracle, unbelievably in love.

Now I realize that this is an extreme case, and I still think she was crazy for staying when she was a punching bag (other battered wives don't always have the same results), but there's no denying her joy.

So the question is, when (if ever) do you pull the plug, or walk out, or quit your job? How long do you hang in there?

The answer? I don't know. I can't play God. I can't say what's best in your situation. Only you can answer that question.

God's Word says, "Let us not get tired of doing what is right, for after a while we will reap a harvest of blessing if we don't get discouraged and give up" (Galatians 6:9).

One Christmas Eve Charlie and I had an argument and I thought that it was the end of love. But then I realized that an argument doesn't necessarily mean the end of love—it's just an argument. I sat down at my desk that night and wrote in big print, "IT'S ALWAYS TOO SOON TO GIVE UP."

That sign is permanently on my desk now. I have forgotten what the argument was about, but the principle remains, it's always too soon to give up.

"Never give up. Never, never!" Those famous words of Winston Churchill could easily be the theme song of a PerSister. She knows that a little more might do it. She keeps getting up again. She's a long hauler. Let's look at three marks of a PerSister.

1. A PerSister Knows a Little More Might Do It

She realizes that the margin of success is often slim . . .
  —just one more sale in the week.
  —just one more vote in the campaign.

—just one more pound on the diet.

—just one more kiss and reconciliation.

Why? Because a breakthrough may be imminent. President Reagan once said, "A hero is no braver than any other individual. He's just brave five minutes longer."

Consider the athletes who compete in the triathlon, the world's most grueling endurance contest. Each year men and women alike start by swimming 2.4 miles battling two-foot waves in the ocean off Hawaii. Then they dry off and bike ride 112 miles over lava fields through gusting headwinds of 25 mph, and conclude with a 26.2-mile marathon while fighting off everything from fatigue and blisters to utter exhaustion and delirium.

Any *one* of those events would do me in, much less all of them. Nevertheless, many athletes are able to finish the entire event, and those who do it in less than nine hours are called Ironmen.

Triathlon world champion David Scott describes his race strategy this way: "It's just a matter of concentration on what you're doing. As soon as you break that concentration, you have lost the race."

When asked, "But how do you maintain that concentration level when you're hurting?" Scott answered, "It's just being able to tolerate a higher level of discomfort. All the stimuli physically and mentally are telling you to stop and there's something way back there that says, 'No, you don't have to stop: keep going, keep going, hold on.'"

The Great Treasure Hunt

In the year 1325 B.C., the young Egyptian pharaoh Tutankhamun died at age eighteen after ruling for nine years.

He was buried in a four-room tomb together with thousands of gold pieces, jewelry, and objects of art.

On November 27, 1922, King Tut's tomb was entered for the first time by British archeologist Howard Carter and his sponsor Lord Carnarvon, who financed the search and expedition.

The story of Carter's search for the tomb is a lesson in persistence. During the nineteenth and early twentieth centuries, treasure hunters and archeologists had vainly searched the Valley of the Kings. Each time they found a tomb, however, they faced disappointment because plunderers through the centuries had ransacked the treasures.

Eventually all of the tombs of the pharaohs were identified, except one—Tutankhamun's, and his treasure promised to be the greatest of all.

Expeditions from around the world began the search in earnest—the Swedes, the Norwegians, the Germans, the French, the Italians, and the Americans.

In 1914, Howard Carter and Lord Carnarvon obtained a concession from the Egyptian government to dig for the tomb. Carter carefully mapped out the entire valley and then began digging methodically down to bedrock, slowly removing thousands of tons of rubble.

The search continued for six separate expeditions over eight years, interrupted by World War I. Finally, only one section of the valley remained to be excavated near the tomb of Rameses II.

The crew began digging. Three days later one man's shovel struck something hard that sounded like concrete.

Excitedly, but carefully, he brushed aside the sand and found a length of cut stone which appeared to be a step.

All of the other team members knelt down to help search for another step. And there was one. And another.

Down, down, down—sixteen steps in all, leading eventually to a doorway filled in with blocks of masonry. The pharaoh's royal seal was impressed in the mortar.

Carefully the team removed one of the blocks, and Howard Carter poked a candle inside. He stuck his head through the opening and let his eyes become adjusted to the darkness. On November 26, 1922, for the first time in over thirty-two centuries, human eyes viewed the pharaoh's treasures which were far greater than any of the search teams had ever imagined.

Joe Blinco in *Decision* magazine tells the rest of the story. When Carter returned to the surface, his colleague Lord Carnarvon asked, "Sir, what did you see?"

"A fabulous treasure," he replied laconically, and began to walk away.

Lord Carnarvon was surprised. He had expected him to be overjoyed at the discovery, but instead he seemed lost in thought.

"What is on your mind?" persisted Lord Carnarvon.

"Twenty years ago," Carter answered slowly, "twenty, dusty, expensive, heartbreaking years ago, I actually began to dig just seventy-two inches east of the place where we found this stone."

Think of it! Twenty years before, only seventy-two more inches would have done it!

Are you about ready to give up? Remember, the margin of success is often slim. You may be only seventy-two inches away.

2. A PerSister Keeps Getting Up Again

Have you ever felt like the world just rolled over on top of you? What do you do when you think you can't go on? Get up and try again. I am encouraged by the following story of someone who did just that.

As a little boy in Ohio, PJ wanted to be in television. He practiced announcing mock broadcasts. He pretended play-by-play of Little League games. He announced homemade horror shows.

But in college and even after graduation, he found no takers for his dream. Station after station told him, "Thanks, but no thanks, you've got an accent." Years went by.

TV station WHIO in Dayton, Ohio, offered PJ the 5:00 A.M. farm reports to give market quotes on soy-beans, corn, and pork bellies. Listeners complained by the droves, "We can't understand him on the air." The station manager tried to improve P.J.'s delivery.

Persistence, persistence, persistence. It was part of PJ's name. He refused to quit and his dream continued to grow. He wanted to host a talk show where viewers would hear opinions from Mrs. Cedar Rapids, Miss Charleston secretary, and middle America. The fact that it hadn't been done before made him even more determined.

His confidence was contagious. Soon the manager caught it. And on November 6, 1967, at 10:30 A.M., PJ (Philip John) Donahue's dream came true, as he launched "The Phil Donahue Show."

To watch him today, it's easy to say, "Sure, he had those gifts all the time—the deep voice, the beautiful hair, the boyish good looks." But more than that he had an idea and determination.

Donahue's confidence also carries over to the studio participants who appear on his show each day. He spends more time with the studio audience before the show than he does with the interview guest.

I remember my excitement when I was first asked to be a Donahue guest. His secretary called to invite me, and I was so thrilled, I almost dropped the phone.

I arrived for the show in Green Bay, Wisconsin, with two friends. We anxiously waited in the Green Room, nervously watching an occasional staff person discuss technical details.

And then Phil came in, or rather rushed in, about nineteen miles per hour. He was wearing a blue pin-stripe suit, and every silver-white hair was in place. He spoke my name and kissed me on the cheek. I felt like I was in a dream. Here was superstar talk host, matinee idol in the flesh!

I heard him say, "Marabel, remember to hit the bottom line. No rambling answers. Get to the point and get off. We've got lots of guests with questions and others who will be calling in. If we get the studio audience involved enough, we've got a winner. I may never get back to you, but that's okay. That's a successful show.

"And one more thing," he said. "Stay away from personal trivia. There's nothing worse than that. One movie star last month said, 'Well I just got back from France making my most recent movie. It rained every day and I missed my plane to Spain.' By that time the studio audience had left to pick up the kids.

"See ya in a moment, kid," and he was gone. Gone to his ladies—his *real* guest stars, his elixir for success, his magic potion.

As I walked into the studio next door, Producer Pat McMillen was speaking to the audience. Then there was laughter and scattered applause as Phil entered from the rear of the set with a mike in his hand. He walked slowly toward the front, asking questions as he came.

"How many of you are pregnant?" he asked. Some hands went up. "How many of you would like to be?" Giggles and laughter. The audience loved it.

He exhorted them to ask questions and participate. "We need you. I'm dead without you. Please help me out. I value your opinions, so don't be afraid to ask questions."

The master was at work, fine-tuning his instruments before the baton came down. He had written the score, but the orchestra this morning was all new. In two minutes, America would tune in to watch his improvisation.

Phil Donahue *is* a master. His guests are incidental and at times almost irrelevant. If a guest ever canceled I believe he could pick a grandmother from the audience and never miss a beat. That's Phil at his best.

A born winner? Not by a long shot. He won by getting up again and again.

3. A PerSister Is a Long-Hauler

As I entered the flower shop, a tall, slim woman behind the counter smiled broadly and called my name. "You don't know who I am, do you?" she asked, with a Cheshire cat grin.

"We were in a sales class together ten years ago," she continued, "don't you remember? I'm Terry."

The class flashed into my mind, and I did remember a

149

Terry—in the back row. But that Terry was enormous, a huge, shapeless mass, and this Terry was tall and lovely.

"Terry!" I shouted. "What happened to you? You look wonderful. What did you do? How did you do it?"

She was delighted to tell me of her success. Over the roses and baby breath, she blurted out her story.

"At age twenty-two, I stopped smoking and began putting on weight—forty-five pounds in six months. It seemed too much to lose. I just lost hope. So I just put on more and more, up to 279 pounds. For seventeen years I was fat."

Terry told of crazy fad diets. She once lost fifty pounds on a liquid diet, but when she started eating normally again, the weight came right back on.

I interrupted, "But you're so thin! What turned the tide?"

"I worked on the Grand Jury for eighteen months. These beautiful and single FBI men came to testify every day, but they never once looked at me. No one ever looked my way. It was as if I didn't even exist. I thought I would never marry. I wanted desperately to be invited to parties. I wanted men to look at me and whistle, not laugh.

"I was never happy fat," Terry continued, "and one day I decided that I could lose it. I looked at myself in the mirror, imagined what I would look like thin, and I determined to do it."

There was one other large woman on the Grand Jury, and Terry asked her one day, "Do you want to see how much we can lose?"

The two of them started.

In six months, Terry lost eighty-five pounds on a diet of salad and baked chicken. Her friend dropped out, but Terry kept going.

She lost her first thirty-five pounds before anyone noticed.

She told me, "Each week or two, I'd take in my clothes so they'd fit. But since I was wearing the same clothes, no one knew I was on a diet.

"One day I let down my hair, put on jeans and heels, and went to work. No one recognized me! Some guy said, 'Hey, whatever happened to that heavy-set girl who used to deliver the stuff?' I answered, 'That's me!' He about fell over. It was great!"

"But did you ever blow it, Terry?" I asked.

"Of course, I blew it sometimes. But then I'd look at myself again and try to picture what I was going to look like. I would tell myself, 'OK, you blew it today. Now start fresh tomorrow.' When you fail, you want to binge. So it's a lifetime battle. The exact same battle routine over and over."

She grinned with pride. "I am not a loser, I have to win. Getting thin was such fun. I had to buy a complete new wardrobe. What a bonus! New stockings, new bras. I even got a fur—a Russian ermine. It was second hand, but to me it was just wonderful."

"And how about those handsome FBI men?"

"Oh, I'm glad you asked," she said. "One day we indicted a judge, and the FBI man we called 'Stonewall' because he never spoke, came back to testify. When he saw me, his mouth fell open. He smiled at me and said, 'Good morning!' I was thrilled beyond words."

Terry beamed her beautiful, radiant smile, and said, "I'd rather be dead than put the weight back on. Now I am the woman I always wanted to be."

Elihu Root said, "Men do not fail. They give up trying." I would love for Mr. Root to meet Terry. She's a PerSister if I ever saw one.

Master Mind

A number of years ago in a large southeastern city, the master composer and pianist, Paderewski, was scheduled to perform. The city was alive with anticipation of this great musician coming to town.

Finally the day arrived. The atmosphere was electric as guests filed into the great concert hall, the men in their black tuxedos and the women in their beautiful ball gowns.

In the crowd that evening was a mother clutching the hand of her young son. Although he had not wanted to come, she had brought him to the concert hoping that if he could just hear the master, perhaps he would be inspired to practice.

When they found their seats, he squirmed and complained. His mother prayed, "Oh, please let the concert begin!"

She turned her head just once to look at a grand lady floating by, and the boy saw his chance. Quick as a flash, he was out of his seat and down the row. He darted into the aisle where he was swept along with the milling throng.

Just at that moment the spotlights began to play on the great Steinway grand onstage, and he was fascinated. He had never before seen such a huge piano.

No one noticed a little boy climbing the steps to the stage. No one noticed a little boy climbing onto the black tufted piano stool. No one noticed, until he raised his little fingers to the keyboard and began to pound out "Chop-sticks."

Suddenly the noise in the auditorium ceased as hundreds of angry faces turned toward the stage. And then the audience began to shout, "Who's that child? Get him out of here! Where's his mother? Who would bring a child to a concert like this?"

Backstage, the master heard the tumult—and "Chopsticks." Realizing what had happened, he grabbed his coat and rushed on stage.

Without a word, he bent down behind the little boy and, with his hands on either side of the boy's, began to compose a counter melody to compliment and enhance "Chopsticks."

As they played together, the master whispered in the little boy's ear, "Keep on. Don't stop. Don't quit. Keep on."

And that's the way it is with us. *The* Master stands behind us and whispers in our ear, "Keep on. Don't stop. Don't quit. Keep on."

3

Sharing with Others

Four Tips for Tired Mothers, Lovers, and Others

1. Lift
2. Laugh
3. Listen
4. Love

Four Tips for Tired Mothers, Lovers, and Others

The bride glowed with happiness, and the groom beamed with pride as the minister smiled, "God must really love you two. You have each been through a lot of pain, but now He's given you a second chance."

Just looking at the two of them gave me a thrill. I wanted their glow to rub off on Charlie and me.

As Joanne and Peter said good-bye to the guests and drove away, I was caught up in their joy. I thought back to my honeymoon and remembered the bliss.

Our wedding ceremony began at 4:00 P.M. When the reception and the endless photographs were finished, a friend who was a policeman drove us to our car parked several miles away (we weren't taking any chances).

Charlie headed for a hotel on Ft. Lauderdale beach like a man possessed. I hadn't eaten all day and was starved to death. "Where are we going to eat?" I asked eagerly.

"Eat?" he repeated. "How can you think of food at a time like this?"

When we finally checked in at our honeymoon hotel, I watched my husband sign, "Mr. and Mrs. Charles Morgan" for the first time. I was wearing my orchid and smiling at everyone in the lobby. The check-in clerk kept staring so I volunteered happily, "We just got married."

"I know," he smiled patronizingly.

What a glorious feeling of relief when the bellman dropped off the bags, ended his extended rundown of all the hotel services available, and finally left.

The door clicked shut. We began married life, our hearts full of love.

One year later, I was sick and tired and pregnant. No longer was I the center of attention as a bride. I dragged myself around trying to bring beauty out of chaos. I felt terrible. Our "Early Halloween" furnishings depressed me. Food nauseated me. Charlie irritated me. He dressed in a crisp suit each morning and trotted off to work at a high-powered law firm where a secretary propositioned him the first day. I was jealous. I felt threatened and angry and fat.

Six years later, I was the full-time parent of two hyperactive little girls. And there was no time for doing my nails or the other little pleasures of life. Dinner hour was a disaster. The kids screamed, the milk spilled, and Charlie didn't talk except to say, "Pass the salt." Afterward, while I cleaned up, Charlie fell asleep in front of the TV. I felt so lonely. I was drowning in downers.

I hesitantly asked some friends about my problems without revealing that I was suffering intensely. One married veteran of thirty-two years of apparent bliss tried to allay my fears. "Don't worry, dear," she said. "Marriage starts out on a high peak of libido, but in a few short years it gradually falls off into a more settled and mature love. It's nothing unusual. It's inevitable."

I couldn't *wait*. She seemed happy, but it certainly wasn't what I had in mind. As I looked at my husband in his comatose state in front of the TV and thought of the dishes and kids that kept calling my name, I said to myself, "That's what we've got all right, settled love." And I didn't like it one bit.

Evolution of a Marriage

If you are married, think back to your honeymoon. Then if you've made it this far, consider your one-year anniversary. And then, if you're still hanging in there, reflect on your five-year (or ten-year) milestone. Do you fit into the evolutionary process on the following chart?

HONEYMOON	ONE YEAR LATER	TEN YEARS LATER
Romantic restaurant	Wendy's	TV dinners
Late-night pizza	Late-night feedings	Late-night fights
Romance	Sex	One-Minute Manager
Exotic travel	Drive to shopping center	Read *National Geographic*
Sizzle	Piddle	Fizzle
Soft, sweet nothings	Sweet nothings	Nothings
Wild bull	Sitting bull	Bull
Passion	Apathy	Atrophy
The Newlywed Game	Family Feud	The Gong Show
Aphrodisiac	Aspirin	Nyquil
Penoir	Bathrobe	Fatigues
Fresh roses	Silk roses	Rose hips
Strawberries & cream	Pickled herring	Grapes of Wrath

Once Upon a Marriage

If I were to ask you to describe your marriage in five words or less, what would you say?

I asked several friends this question. Joanne, the two-week newlywed, just smiled and crooned, "Wonderful, wonderful, wonderful!"

Then I asked Debbie, the almost-divorcee, the same question, "What is a marriage?"

"Yours or mine?" she asked. Then she added, "Mine is spelled D-I-S-A-S-T-E-R."

I really wasn't asking for a definition of *her* marriage, but she was so affected personally that she couldn't define the word objectively. Her perception of marriage in general was tainted by her own personal experience. But then, of course, that's true of all of us who are married, or were, or would like to be.

At the wedding of Britain's Prince Charles and Lady Diana, Dr. Robert Runcie, Archbishop of Canterbury, told the royal couple, "Our faith sees the wedding day not as the place of arrival, but the place where the adventure really begins."

What is this animal called marriage? Is it a savage beast or a pussycat? Each of us comes at it from a different angle. One feels warmth and strength. Another thinks she has a stray. And still another feels she was ripped apart by this monster. Is marriage all of the above, or none of the above?

Marriage is probably the most fragile of all relationships. More fragile than the parent-child because it is not a blood relationship. And more fragile than a business partnership because sex and love are involved.

Several years ago I was given a beautiful crystal bowl

which I used only on very special occasions. One day while I was drying the bowl, it leaped out of my hands and shattered into a million pieces. I felt shattered, too.

The marriage vessel is as fragile as that bowl. It can self-destruct with a word, a look, a misunderstanding. Damage done in an instant may take days to heal (or months or years).

Destruction is not necessarily divorce. We all know of marriages that are dead de facto, but are kept alive socially. They are destroyed nevertheless.

The theory expressed in the amusing chart on the Evolution of a Marriage is pretty discouraging, especially for a young bride starting off on this matrimonial road. The message to her is, "Enjoy while you can, because this is the best you're going to get. It's all downhill from here."

Or is it? Must it be? Is there any reason why a five-year anniversary or a fifteen-year anniversary can't have sizzle and excitement and high adventure?

And what about the kids? If Mom and Dad aren't doing well, must the kids suffer, too? Are they doomed to oblivion in front of the TV because Mom can't cope?

How can a woman balance her roles as a wife, mother, home executive, and/or career woman? The same way a tightrope walker crosses Niagara Falls while juggling eight crystal plates.

Very carefully. Very, very carefully.

Even if your marriage road is rocky, I believe you can have a revolution in your evolution. In the next four chapters I would like to share with you four tips for tired mothers, lovers, and others. I hope they will be helpful in turning those negative charges into a positive current that will light up your life.

9

LIFT

One Saturday morning recently, Michelle and I watched the launch of a space shuttle on TV.

Countdown—10, 9, 8, 7, 6, 5, 4, 3 . . . Lift off.

Clouds of smoke and fire. The earth shook, the sky was ablaze, the roar was heard for miles, as the rocket headed up and out of sight.

I was awed. What power. We sat in silence listening to the radio reports from the crew. A TV reporter gave facts. "The satellite and module weigh 92 million tons."

"Incredible," I said to Michelle. "How in the world is it possible for all that weight to lift into space?

"Simple, Mom," she chirped.

"Simple? Are you kidding?"

"It's just Newton's Third Law of Motion. Nothing to it."

One thing I can't stand is a smart kid. But it's a little easier when it's my own.

I felt so dumb in asking, "OK, so what's the Third Law of Whatever Whoever?" Then, somewhat amazed, I listened as she quickly explained.

"For every action, there's an equal and opposite reaction. The rocket first forces power downward, then the equal and opposite reaction powers the missile upward. The greater the force, the more powerful the launch power. That's what causes it to lift off."

My little professor continued her physics cram course, "It's the same principle with a tennis ball, Mom. What happens when you throw it against a wall? It comes back just as hard."

I could see that Newton's law of physics also applies in everyday life. Throw a smile at the sullen waitress and watch a smile come back. Conversely, snap at her for your luke-warm soup and you'd better duck.

Jesus recited this same law long before Newton. We call it The Golden Rule. "Do unto others as you would have them do unto you." This implies that people will respond in the same manner in which they have received.

In his book, *Keys to the Kingdom,* Pat Robertson, host of "The 700 Club," calls this the "Law of Reciprocity." As you give, so shall you receive. It's a law of human nature, just as true as the physical laws of the universe.

Launching Love

Try it. Launch a little love today—not only with your friends or family, but also in an unloving environment. Stepping out and being the first to show love is always tough.

The risk is obvious and predictable. What if he (or she) doesn't love me back?

I mentioned this Law of Reciprocity on a TV panel talk show in New York City. Another guest interrupted, "Why should I lower myself and show love first? What about him? Let him start. Why don't you go tell my husband this trash about 'launching love'?"

After the show a psychiatrist called the station and asked to speak to me. He said, "Don't be intimidated by that woman. Your principle works. She doesn't understand that it takes a strong person to initiate a cycle of behavior. Giving love first is not weakness; it's a show of strength."

Launching Hope

In a small town in the Soviet Union, a minister was arrested for preaching in an underground church. This was not his first offense; he had been warned before, but he could not keep silent. He was sentenced to a concentration camp in Siberia.

His closest friend back home was a barber who was heartbroken over the arrest. After several weeks of mourning, the barber traveled to Siberia and applied for a job in the prison camp. He was assigned to cut the hair of the prisoners.

The barber's new job was tedious—cutting hair while a soldier stood watch. But he worked with the hope that one day his friend would be brought in for a haircut.

After weeks and weeks the day finally arrived, but because of the prison guard, the only thing the barber could say to his friend was, "Sir, keep your chin up."

Again, several months later, he repeated the haircut and the advice, "Sir, keep your chin up. Keep your chin up, Sir."

Over the three and a half years that followed, the barber spoke to his friend only a few times. But each time those same encouraging words gave the pastor the courage to keep going.

The Perfect Lift

The word *encourage* means to give courage, to inspire with courage, to give hope, hearten, cheer up or on. The opposite of encouragement is discouragement, which often takes the form of criticism.

A tough radio talk-show hostess was surprised recently when a caller on her program said, "Good morning, nice lady."

Taken aback, she responded, "Well, good morning to you, nice man." She was kind and courteous to the caller throughout the conversation which lasted several minutes. She didn't display her typical cutting demeanor. Why? The Law of Reciprocity had worked.

Remember the words of John Bunyan? "A man there was and they called him mad. The more he gave, the more he had."

Do you know what's the greatest gift you can give a person? Or the perfect gift for someone who has everything? The most appreciated yet least expensive gift in the world is a word of encouragement. The lift-gift, given over the years by the truly great.

Catherine II of Russia said, "I praise loudly; I blame softly."

Robert Louis Stevenson advised, "Keep your fears to yourself, share your courage with others."

A simple word of encouragement has been known to work worlds of wonders. Here are four wonders of the world.

1. ENCOURAGEMENT GIVES A START

Who gave you your first break? A very special teacher? A tenth-grade girlfriend? A demanding piano instructor? Or a dedicated coach?

Think back, recall the people who influenced your life in a specific way. These probably are the most unforgettable people in your life. Why? Because they believed in you and saw a glimmer of potential. They cared enough to give you a word of encouragement.

I will never forget the encouragement of a kind sophomore girl when I was a freshman in high school. Because of my home situation, I had wandered through junior high in a daze locked in my own little shell. Now in the huge high school, I had very few friends. Most noontimes I ate lunch alone, sitting at the end of a table in the cafeteria longingly observing the uproarious activity of all the students.

One cold day in February just before noon, as we cleaned up our desks in art class, a popular sophomore leaned over and asked, "Marabel, would you like to eat lunch with us today?"

I was both thrilled and scared—thrilled because she wanted me to sit with her, but apprehensive because Margie was the Homecoming Queen, the darling of our school. What if she wouldn't like me? What if I dribbled my milk?

That she would even look in my direction was unbeliev-able to me. But when I sat at her table that day, I felt loved and wanted, no longer an outcast, but part of a group, the inner circle.

Several big upperclassmen boys sauntered by and spoke to the girls at the table. One tossed his banana peel on my tray. My heart leaped. The crowning touch. I had been accepted.

My love and gratitude for Margie were limitless. I had felt alone for years, and when she included me, it was a turning point in my life. From then on I ate lunch with friends each day. I learned how to talk and interact with people. That little act of kindness, the invitation to lunch, gave me a sense of belonging. Her lift gave me a start. Thank you, Margie.

The simple act of encouragement can be expressed through a compliment, or a word of praise, or even through a friendly nickname you call your friends.

A number of years ago in Australia, two young boys wanted to learn to play tennis. Harry Hopman, a local coach, saw them struggling to hit the ball. He noticed that neither had much natural ability—one was slow, and the other was weak. But he wanted to encourage them so he gave them positive nicknames. The slow one he called "Rocket," and the weak one he called "Muscles."

In just a few short years, those two young men, Ken "Muscles" Rosewall and Rod "Rocket" Laver, went on to become the superstars of professional tennis around the world.

You, too, can be the starter in someone else's life. Today, look for potential and tap it. A brief word of encouragement said in passing may be the very thing that starts someone in a new direction. Remember, small beginnings can have long-lasting results.

2. ENCOURAGEMENT GIVES HOPE

One weekend recently, I played golf with Charlie. I am the first to admit that I'll never win the U.S. Open, but Charlie loves for me to play and is remarkably patient with me while I'm learning.

On one hole, when I hit a drive into the woods, Charlie exclaimed, "That's all right, Honey, you *almost* caught that one!"

That's a nice way of saying, "What a lousy shot, but at least you tried." I appreciated his word of encouragement, and somehow it softened the embarrassment of the horrible shot. It also inspired me to try harder on the next hole, and to my surprise, my next drive was much better.

I have received letters from women all over the country looking for hope. I call these the "Help Wanted" letters. They are all quite similar in form.

Here is one from North Dakota: "My husband is stationed 2,000 miles from here and he seldom calls. I asked him if there was another woman; he said 'No.' I also asked if my being overweight had anything to do with his lack of interest; he said 'No.' Do you think there is hope for our marriage even though we're separated?"

I feel that one of my missions in life is to give hope through encouragement, and thereby motivate a woman to action. Once she believes there is hope, she can map out a plan to accomplish her goals.

Sometimes just "being there" is all you can do, but it is enough if it gives hope.

The story is told of a salesman who hadn't made a sale in months. His debts were enormous. His marriage was falling apart. He saw no way out except suicide.

One day, he confided to an assistant at work that he was planning to take his life. His assistant was shocked, but calmly said, "Oh, that's such a lonely way. You can't go through that alone. I'll stand by you. I'll go with you to your lawyer. I'll go with you when you kiss your wife and little ones good-bye. And I'll stay with you at the end to comfort you."

The man was overwhelmed. He said, "If someone cares *that much* about me, then life must be worth living."

That assistant was a hope dispenser. You and I can be hope dispensers, too.

3. ENCOURAGEMENT GIVES CONFIDENCE

Psychologist Anne Moliver Ruben of Miami Beach, author of *How I Grew Up to Be a Happy Child,* says, "Confident children are happy children because they feel good about themselves. They meet each day with optimism. They are not afraid to make decisions."

Dr. Ruben stresses the importance of praising good behavior. She advises, "Tell your child, 'I'm so proud of how well you got along with your sister today.' This not only reinforces positive behavior, but also builds self-confidence."

More than three million American children between the ages of six and thirteen come home from school each day to an empty house. No parent is at home. These so-called "latchkey" kids (plus an estimated 50,000 preschoolers) fend for themselves while their parents are occupied in the work place.

A child's mind is like a computer. Who is programming these children to be self-confident? Other playmates? The television? Hardly. How vital it is that the working mother give her children encouragement when she returns home at the end of the day!

At times the very nature of our high-tech world erodes the confidence of all of us. Husbands, friends—*every*body benefits from an encouraging word.

4. ENCOURAGEMENT GIVES AN EXAMPLE

Last Saturday I set out in search of four kitchen chairs. I went to three different stores before I finally found the right chair at a large furniture discount center.

I told the salesman, "I'll take four."

"Just a minute, lady, I'll have to see if we still have any in stock. Wait for me at that long counter and I'll see you shortly."

I wandered back to the waiting area and watched a petite Spanish cashier total a large order. The customer explained how his payments would have to be arranged. I wondered how the cashier would decipher the eight pages of fine print posted on the wall behind her marked, "Important Information Concerning Financing." The intricate government regulations, company financing policy, disclosure forms, and interest schedules were beyond me. *Surely she'll call the manager,* I thought.

But the ninety-eight-pound Cuban dynamo proved me wrong. She pulled out a blank form and placed it next to another form marked "Sample Completed Form." Quickly she filled in the lines and in three minutes was finished.

Amazing, I thought to myself. If I had had to read all of that fine print, I would be out of a job. I couldn't read it in the first place; I couldn't understand it in the second.

But show me an example and it's a snap. A good example is more effective than a formal treatise and easier to follow than an essay.

Show me a teacher who makes chemistry exciting, and I'll head back to the science lab.

Show me a mother who understands her child's special needs, and I'll throw away ten books on child rearing to play with my kids instead.

And show me a Friend (the Supreme Example) who loves me enough to listen to my complaints,

> —to comfort me when I hurt,
> —to give me direction and guidance,
> —to forgive me when I disappoint,
> —to die for all my wrongs,
> —and I'll follow Him forever.

That dear Supreme Example gave us many words of encouragement. All through Scripture we are exhorted, "Encourage each other to build each other up" (1 Thessalonians 5:11).

You and I can do it! We can make a difference in our little world. Join the League of Hope Dispensers. Even as a brand new member, you can defuse angry words in your house, you can pacify irate shopkeepers, clients, and neighbors. You can change the depressing atmosphere of double downers by lifting yourself to a level of life electrically charged with *joy!* All this with an encouraging word.

10

LAUGH

I headed for the checkout lane, squeaky cart piled high with boxes and bottles, and a few dozen junk food extras that thirteen-year old Michelle had sneaked in under the paper towels.

I turned into the first lane, and caught a glimpse of the checkout girl. Cashier #1 resembled a Marine drill sergeant, hard and stout, arms tightly folded. As she glared at me, her cold stare said, "I dare you to come in here!"

And I didn't. I kept the basket rolling.

I glanced down the next two aisles. Cashier #2 was "Miss Dead-on-Her-Feet." She was dozing while leaning against the cash register. I thought, *It must have been a late one last night.* It would have been cruel to wake her, so I pushed on to the last aisle.

My eyes met Cashier #3. She was alive. "Come on over," she sang out. "I've never seen the place this empty."

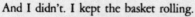

Leanne

I felt relieved. Before I could see her name badge, she smiled, "Hi, my name is Leanne."

"Did you just move here?" I asked.

"Well, I came here for the summer. I'm a sophomore at Florida State."

Her eyes danced as she told Michelle and me of her freshman year. All six hands were unloading raisins, bacon, peanut butter, apples, and pineapples without even looking down. Buying groceries had never been so pleasant.

We laughed, caught up with each other. Instant friends. Leanne bagged the last box of napkins and set the eggs gently on top, and we said, "Good-bye."

The automatic doors opened and I pushed out into the parking lot.

"Why can't life be one long checkout in Aisle #3?" I asked Michelle as I started the car. "Why can't we be like Leanne, giving joy to every dreary and unsuspecting customer who comes along?"

"We can!" shouted Michelle. "We can!"

I don't want to go through life as a drill sergeant or half asleep. I want to live life in the fun lane. Here's how.

1. LAUGHTER MAKES THE MUNDANE SPECIAL

Remember Mary Poppins, the nanny with the umbrella who approached every mundane task with fun? While watching her work, one of her incorrigible little charges exclaimed, "I get it! It's a game, isn't it?"

As Mary Poppins danced and dusted around the room, she

explained that it all depends on your point of view. You can find some fun in every job.

Mary Poppins' enthusiasm swept America. Soon everybody was singing to lighten their load, "Just a spoonful of sugar helps the medicine go down, in the most delightful way!"

Most women I know don't need encouragement to celebrate holidays. Almost everyone gets excited at Christmas and Thanksgiving and on birthdays. But what about the months and months of monotony in between? The ho-hum Tuesdays? The ordinary, humdrum days?

I believe it doesn't take any more time or money to make the mundane exciting. All it takes is a little imagination and a "fun" attitude. Your *attitude* can transform tonight's dinner into a happening.

Celebrate!

Celebrate Tuesdays, Sundays, half birthdays!

Celebrate haircuts, new jeans, report cards.

Celebrate braces on, braces off.

Celebrate if Daddy comes home early.

Celebrate if Daddy comes home!

Since the wife's attitude sets the atmosphere, it is so easy to make happy days. I am a realist and I know that life is a struggle. But you can make your husband and children feel that life is worth living when their days are filled with new experiences and celebrations.

Celebrate with your family tonight. Dress up like the Fourth of July. Light firecrackers. The children will see that you're a fun mommy, and your husband will know that you really care.

Okay, so you can't swing a celebration this week. How

about next week? Plan ahead for Thursday. And try to celebrate at least once a week.

Do you know what it takes to celebrate? Stick a candle in the meatloaf. Instant celebration! Tint the mashed potatoes pink! Make your husband's favorite dinner. Jar your family from their lethargy. Put on that Halloween mask. Swing from the chandelier. Eat dinner *under* the dining room table.

Then after Junior goes to bed, move the celebration to the bedroom. Knock your husband's eyeballs out! Celebrate!

And what if he laughs? That's the whole idea.

2. LAUGHTER HELPS TO HEAL

That wise old King Solomon shared a pearl of wisdom, "A cheerful heart does good like medicine, but a broken spirit makes one sick." Medical research shows that a happy person has definite healing qualities within.

In his book, *Laugh After Laugh: The Healing Power of Humor*, Psychologist Raymond Moody shows how psychiatrists have confirmed the truth of Solomon's verse medically. Dr. Moody gives examples of patients who have "laughed themselves back to health, or at least have used their sense of humor as a positive and adaptive response to their illness." Humor and laughter, he writes, "have long been thought to be health giving."

As an experiment, Dr. Moody took a clown into a psychiatric ward and carefully observed the reactions of patients. He discovered a remarkably high recovery rate among those who began to laugh. Humor healed.

In one counseling case, Moody tells of a gloomy, depressed patient who had worked in a cookie factory. One day the patient arrived even more discouraged than usual. That week, his new foreman had ordered an increase in cookie production, but the employee knew that the wrapping machine couldn't handle the increased capacity.

Still the supervisor insisted on the increase. So the employee reluctantly turned on the machine to its highest level and watched apprehensively as the machine roared into action. Within minutes cookies started shooting everywhere. An avalanche of cookies spewed out machine-gun style.

The supervisor screamed at the employee and blamed him for the fiasco. An unjust double downer for the conscientious employee who had warned his boss about this very problem!

The vicious reprimand continued while the pile of cookies formed around their feet. Dr. Moody began to picture the runaway cookie machine. He tried to hold back his laughter, but the corners of his mouth began to turn up. As he bit his lip, his distraught patient saw his smile.

To his amazement, the patient also began to smile. Suddenly, the two of them broke out into peals of laughter.

That moment became the turning point in the patient's therapy. "Standing back from his life situation and seeing it from a comic—even cosmic—perspective," writes Moody, "he realized that he had been playing a game with himself."

The patient saw that he could remove himself from this troubling situation. He applied for a management-training position and soon was transferred into a more congenial atmosphere.

Physicians in various fields now confirm the beneficial side effects of laughter. Doctor Sharon Begley, writing on the "Biology of Laughter," explains, "A hardy laugh produces well-documented physical effects, many of them akin to moderate exercise. Muscles in the abdomen, chest, shoulders and elsewhere contract, heart rate and blood pressure increase. In a paroxysm of laughter, the pulse can double from 60 to 120, and systolic blood pressure can shoot from a norm of 120 to a very excited 200."

Psychologist Jeffrey Goldstein of Temple University in the Sciences, writes, "It is not too farfetched that laughter is related in several ways to longevity"—mainly through the reduction of stress and hypertension.

Learn to laugh. It's the least expensive medicine around.

3. LAUGHTER IS CONTAGIOUS

Once I asked a prominent Southern hostess the secret of her successful parties. "Your parties are the highlight of the year," I told her. "What makes them so special?"

"I try to invite only happy and fun-loving people," she confided. "I keep track of different types of people and eliminate the complainers and grumblers."

Since then, I've noticed that happy people stand out even in a crowd. They seem to look younger than they really are. And before long their happiness seems to spread to others. People want to be around happy people.

In Michelle's history class one day, two of her friends started giggling over a whispered secret. Within a few minutes their desks were shaking from their laughter. Others across the aisle couldn't help noticing, and they, too, started

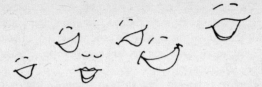

laughing. Shortly the entire class, including her stern teacher, all joined in.

Laughter is contagious. Haven't you seen travel pictures of a snaggletoothed native from a South Sea island? Even though the poor soul is weather beaten, your heart responds involuntarily to his wide smile and the sparkle in his eye.

One night, Charlie and I stood in the bedroom, eye to eye and nose to nose (almost!) arguing over a leak in the water line. (We have more problems with our water!) He was mad, not only because he thought the plumber had charged an outrageous price, but also because I had paid the bill.

When I defended the plumber, Charlie jumped all over me. I got mad, and within minutes the fur was flying.

Suddenly it struck me, "This is crazy! Here we are, husband and wife. We are both on the same side. We both want the leak fixed. So how did the plumber and I get thrown together?" My dear, frustrated husband, who was turning red in the face, had lost his perspective, and so had I.

I thought to myself, *Our relationship is too important to let some dumb plumber come between us!* I looked at Charlie and smiled. I began to laugh out loud. He smiled slightly because I was *really* laughing.

By this time Charlie was sitting on the bed, and he tentatively began to laugh. He looked so puzzled that I collapsed against the wall. Charlie looked at me and laughed so hard that the bed shook. That really set us off. And after we could laugh no longer, we were able to talk about the plumber.

All throughout the evening, whenever we looked at each other we smiled. Our laughter had eased the tense situation and we felt so close.

Incredible, I thought. Just an hour before we had wanted to claw each other's eyes out and now we felt this special, secret bond.

Dr. William F. Fry, Jr., associate clinical professor of psychiatry at Stanford University School of Medicine, writes, "Psychiatrists have long known that humor is emotionally stimulating, and that sharing laughter is a way to enhance intimacy."

Think of that! Laughter helps to lighten your load and serves as a positive reinforcement, drawing two hearts together. For some reason the world seems less difficult to face with a smile on your face.

Laughter is like a bottled lotion, good only when opened and applied. Start spreading it. You'll be surprised at how far it reaches.

4. LAUGHTER MAKES THE UNBEARABLE BEARABLE

Carol is one of those people who can find humor in anything. Dunk her under water, and she'll come up blowing bubbles. You can't drown her spirit.

She was Charlie's secretary for a year before her husband, George, moved the family to Alaska. No job was lined up, but he felt that electricians were needed for the pipeline, so off they went.

A month later, Carol's first letter to the office arrived. Tons of disappointments to be sure, but she hadn't forgotten how to laugh.

Here are parts of her letter. To separate the adverse conditions from Carol's running commentary, I have split it into two columns.

Dear Ones:

THE FACTS

THE FUN

I cried and cried the day I left. It was so hard for me to bear. My eyes were swollen for days.

The trip was rough and long. I wasn't thrilled about Montana or Wyoming—BORING and UGLY. George kept stopping to take pictures of deer and moose.

Only one problem—most of the pictures were of their backends because they started running as soon as the van stopped. So we have a lot of "behind pictures" of those animals.

We went to the salmon spawning area—something to behold. George was impressed.

All I saw were those poor, old, tired, motionless fish, just sort of sitting around. What a life!?!?

THE FACTS	THE FUN
Not much to do at night. I've taken up Bunka.	It's a wild and crazy Alaskan dance. Just kidding. It's a type of Oriental embroidery and I love it. Am doing a cockatoo rooster with long tails.
I'm working part time for a church where the pastor is fighting a bar next door from staying open longer hours.	I just had two obscene phone calls from a drunk wanting to know if the pastor was a pervert!
Keep in touch and pray.	And as we go up together, don't get your wing caught in mine. I think mine will be a little tangled. (Gabriel thought I was going to walk up instead of fly, so he left mine packed away and it got all matted.)
Love, Carolcitabombitananacita.	You can take the girl out of Miami, but you can't take all the Cuban out of the girl—even in Alaska!

Carol has a gift of making fun. Not fun *of* people, but fun *in spite of* people and circumstances. That is not always an easy exercise. Everyone I know with that gift seems to enjoy life more than the masses. And the masses in turn respond. Everyone loves a laugher.

So often I forget how to laugh at myself. I take myself far too seriously. When troubles hit like a ton of bricks, I see more mud than stars.

What's so much fun about going to the dry cleaners? Or grocery shopping? Or doing dishes? Fun is reserved for the party Friday night! Right?

Wrong! Why wait for the party? Why not have fun right now, in this moment?

Beverly Sills was asked one day why she always seemed so happy, in spite of deep family tragedies and personal sorrow. "Happy?" she repeated. "No. Cheerful? Yes."

That's the difference. The big difference lies in whether one chooses to be miserable or triumphant.

My friend Julie recently had a breast removed. She lives in a northern city, and I was sorry that I could not visit her.

Several days later she called. Before I could even worry about how to broach the question, she opened, "This is your one-breasted paper-hanger calling!" What a sense of humor!

Julie is coping very well. She is a living example that laughter makes the unbearable bearable.

Drew's Law of Human Biology says, "The first bug to hit the windshield lands directly in front of your eyes."

When you see the bug, look for the laugh.

11

LISTEN

One rainy day when I was in junior high school, our phys ed class played a game called "Telephone." We sat on the gym floor in circles of ten and one girl whispered a secret to the girl sitting next to her. She then whispered it to her neighbor, and on and on around the circle. The final message was always worlds removed from what the first girl had whispered.

Author Chuck Swindoll told a humorous story of how a message became garbled when it was told and retold at a Marine base.

The colonel issued this directive to his executive officer: "Tomorrow evening at approximately 2000 hours, Halley's Comet will be visible in this area, an event which occurs once every seventy-five years. Have the men fall out in the battalion area in fatigues, and I will explain this rare phenomenon to them. In case of rain we will not be able to see anything, so assemble the men in the theater and I will show them films of it."

The executive officer then told the company commander:

"By order of the colonel, tomorrow at 2000 hours, Halley's Comet will appear above the battalion area. If it rains, fall the men out in fatigues; then march to the theater where the rare phenomenon will take place, something which occurs only once every seventy-five years."

The company commander in turn told the lieutenant:

"Tomorrow at 2000 hours, the colonel, in fatigues, will appear in the theater with Halley's Comet, something which happens every seventy-five years. If it rains, the colonel will order the comet into the battalion area."

And finally the sergeant told his squad:

"When it rains tomorrow at 2000 hours, the phenomenal seventy-five-year-old General Halley, accompanied by the colonel, will drive his Comet through the battalion area theater in fatigues."

What confusion! When one fails to listen, the message is distorted and the listener goes away bewildered.

So little energy is required to listen carefully to another human being, but it's a service with long-lasting benefits.

Often I work at my kitchen sink with the phone cradled to my ear, listening to friends who call. Some of them men and young teenage girls—runaways. People hungry for someone to care and to listen.

Of course my top priority as a wife and mother is to be available to listen to my own husband and children when they need me.

A wise friend once told me, "If you listen to your children when they're little, they'll still be talking when they're teenagers."

That advice kept me steady through months and months of unceasing chatter from a seven-year-old. One afternoon I spent twenty minutes hanging on her every word about some hermit crab crawling up the screen door. It almost drove me crazy. Not just the ponderous details about the art of crab-crawling on screens, but I had *important* things to do. Still I listened.

Today my darling is fifteen and we are talking woman-to-woman. I am eager to hang on every word, even though I'm not into whether Angie's dating Chris (or was it Alfred or Jaimie?), or what Beth is wearing to the party. Her interests interest me. I want to know what's going on in her brain, how she's meeting the challenges of her day, and how she feels about herself. She's been talking all these years rather incessantly, and it appears that the trend is not about to end.

It takes sacrifice to listen, Mom, but it's worth it. Be available when they want you. You only have a few short years and then they're gone.

Communication Avenue is a two-way street, capable of handling traffic from either direction. The problem comes when someone wants to make it one-way and usurps the other lane. Then it's just a matter of time until a collision occurs, or the other driver finds a detour to another street.

Keep Communication Avenue open with no obstructions. Kids love that highway. So do husbands and friends and others who turn onto it.

Listeners of the Lost Art

Do you know one of the secrets of being a successful talk-show host? Most of the really good ones are better listeners than they are talkers. They have learned to listen and draw out their guests. This secret is effective in everyday life, as well as on a talk show.

The gift of listening is a very special quality. Everyone loves a good listener. Why? Because the listener makes the one doing the talking feel important. On the other hand, the egocentric, nonstop bore doesn't communicate interest or concern for anyone.

At the next function you attend, watch for the overbearing, bragging showoff, then watch the crowds thin out in disgust as the speaker begins to rise in his or her self-aggrandizement.

Here are four tips on how to be your own talk-show host all day long.

1. DON'T SHOW SHOCK OR BIAS

I learn this lesson from experience daily. When four people—four *volatile* people—live together, great energy and wisdom is needed to provide even brief moments of harmony.

Sweet bliss can be shattered by one word. Yesterday is a case in point. Laura and I were chattering happily at Sunday breakfast when she began to tell me a shocking story about some friends of hers. I was appalled. I interrupted her story before she had finished and began to moralize.

"Forget it, Mom," she said annoyed. "I'm not the one who needs the lecture."

I was not content to leave well enough alone, but tried to drive my point further. Laura was offended and started to defend the outrageous behavior, saying that I didn't know all the facts. Suddenly we were shouting at each other, and she stormed out of the kitchen. I knew I wouldn't be able to pry the rest of the story out with a crowbar.

Although it requires great control to stay cool in the face of radical statements issuing from one's children, I could have kept Communication Avenue open.

By the time we left for church, I was feeling blue. I knew that the tension between Laura and me could ruin our Sunday and it was all my fault. I feared the estrangement could hang on for days.

I told myself, *Life is too short for this.* Emotions and situations can be redeemed. As vital as listening is the fine art of touching. I patted Laura's arm as we walked into church and whispered, "I'm so very sorry for getting on your case." She didn't respond, but I knew she would think about it and soften eventually.

Later when she was folding clothes (an indication to me that she wanted to show responsibility), I came by and grinned, "I need a hug."

That little line is a signal we use when we want to make amends. It helps save face and soothe away the tension. It almost always works.

One parenthetical word of warning is needed. Not only must parents keep their mouths shut when the kids are sharing intimately, they also need to keep their confidences afterward. If they reveal, you conceal. Don't break the confidence.

Look at the successful talk-show host. He appears neutral on issues. He doesn't show his bias, and even the questions he asks don't necessarily reveal his personal position.

Shock or disapproval may stop a conversation cold. A judgmental attitude may show up in many ways. Facial expressions, a stern tone of voice, or a wild frenzy in the eye can be read as negative signals by someone who is looking for any clue to stop talking.

Of course, the heart cry of every wife is that her husband will share his innermost thoughts with her. So remember, if you want the other party to talk—be it your child, your husband, or your friend—keep your feelings to yourself during the story. Bite your tongue if necessary. After all these years, that's why mine's just a stub.

2. GIVE YOUR UNDIVIDED ATTENTION

One of my pet peeves is to talk with a person and watch her constantly look past me to others. If she is scouting out the room while pretending to talk to me, I feel like a second-class citizen. She seems to be only enduring me until someone better comes along.

However, I don't always give my undivided attention either. One reason is that we human beings are capable of listening five times faster than we can talk. In other words, we can listen to maybe five hundred words per minute or read as much as five thousand words per minute, but we speak only one hundred words per minute. During a slow or boring presentation concentration obviously is difficult. An active mind can be doing flip-flops and half gainers while the speaker drones on and on.

Is it possible to do several things at once and still hear someone talking? Sure. How many times have you prepared dinner while listening to Sally's school report, with the radio on, and still be thinking about that last conversation with your friend?

But even though I know I can do my kitchen chores while listening to a literature paper, my daughter doubts it. She wants my undivided attention to assure her that I am in fact listening.

When Michelle was ten, I had been unusually busy for several weeks before Christmas. I was caught up with phone calls, appointments, and people stopping by. Michelle followed me around one night while I was cooking, and suddenly I realized I hadn't spoken with her personally for days. She was chattering away and I stopped and said, "Honey, I want to really hear what you're saying. Let's go sit in the living room."

As I looked into her eyes and responded with enthusiasm, she became very vivacious. I could tell she was exhilarated about sitting on the sofa talking, just the two of us, woman to woman.

When she finished her story, I went back to making dinner. In a few minutes, she ran in, hugged me, and said, "Mom, this is the best day of my whole life!"

Your children will believe you're the most wonderful person in the world if you are available to listen to them. Being available is the difficult part. A ninth-grader once told me,

"What's the use of coming home after school? There's no one home, or if Mom is there, she's always on the phone."

It takes time to communicate with your kids, especially as they grow through those turbulent teenage years. Children don't always voice their deepest feelings in the first sentence. They wait to see if Mom or Dad has time to hear them out.

I have discovered a little communication technique that works with children, as well as adults. Children (and others) seem more willing to share their innermost secrets indirectly rather than eyeball to eyeball. Somehow emotions are less intense that way.

When mother and daughter do the dishes together, for example, there is an indirect opportunity for intimate talks. Driving together also enhances family compatibility and communication. And simply sitting on the bed at night in the dark opens the door for conversation from the heart.

But now, with dishwashers and airplanes and demanding social schedules, cozy times have been replaced by the rush of life. While speeding along on today's Twentieth Century Fast Track, it's so easy to fly right by Communication Avenue. If you miss it, slow down and take the next exit called Listener's Lane.

3. Look for Follow-ups

Have you ever tried to start a conversation in a social situation, but for the life of you, couldn't get the ball rolling?

I have, especially if circumstances have thrust me together with a stranger at a long luncheon or committee meeting or business project. Several of my friends say they sometimes experience these same awkward moments when on a date.

A good listener looks for ways to keep the conversation moving. She has several tools in her box: last phrase, paraphrase, feelings, detail, warmth, blind spots, and hot buttons.

• *Last phrase.* Once when Bob Hope was a guest on "The Donahue Show," I watched with great interest as two real pros were face to face. During one story, Bob Hope recounted his entrance into the entertainment world years before. As he talked, I tried to anticipate the follow-up question that Phil Donahue would ask. I made a mental note of five possible questions, all relevant to Mr. Hope's experiences.

But I was surprised by the question that Phil asked. It pertained to the very last phrase that his guest had spoken. There was no way that Phil could have anticipated that last phrase, but he followed up on it because it was the last issue to be mentioned.

Bob Hope was visibly pleased by the question. He had mentioned the phrase in almost a throwaway gesture, but Phil had caught it before it hit the ground and Hope seemed delighted for the opportunity to continue the flow.

If you're stuck in the conversational mud, follow up on the last phrase. You may find yourself right back on track.

• *Paraphrase.* Another discussion prodder is the paraphrase. When the conversation lags, try to summarize earlier thoughts by rephrasing what was just said. "In other words, you're saying . . .?" This also helps check your perception level if the subject matter is complicated. The speaker will then continue on with great gusto.

• *Feelings.* During a lull you might ask, "How did you feel about the election?" Most people love the chance to explain their feelings, especially on volatile subjects. But don't try to *change* those feelings, just hear them out.

• *Detail.* Another sure-fire way for keeping the ball rolling is to ask for details. "Tell me more about those black holes in space." Or, "What did the hermit crab look like? Draw it for me."

Incidentally, I have found that people very rarely grow tired of answering questions. Everyone likes to be considered an expert and is eager to share his or her experiences with anyone who will only listen sincerely.

• *Warmth.* Make your friends feel important. One popular hostess greets her guests with the phrase, "Where have you been? I could hardly wait to see you!" And when they leave, she says, "Oh, so soon?" Who doesn't love to be treated as a special guest?

• *Blind Spots.* Everyone has his or her blind spots. Even King David wrote about his own "hidden faults" in the Psalms. We are so close to the forest that we can't see the trees. We are blind to our own errors, and we can't converse objectively on those subjects.

For that reason, if you want someone to open up with you, beware the blind spots. When you see a defensive look or hear a hostile voice, you've probably hit a sensitive nerve, a blind spot. Move on before the hostility is transferred to you.

• *Hot Buttons.* On the other hand, all of us have our hot buttons. These are not necessarily negative buttons, but favorite topics, too. Buttons that ring our bell. Subjects we love. When someone asks us about these we come alive.

While waiting for Michelle in the doctor's office I saw a

neighbor enter the room. I tried to be friendly, but she seemed so disinterested. Each question I asked fell flat. I began to feel strange myself.

I happened to comment on her tennis outfit, and suddenly she came alive as if she were animated. She couldn't stop talking about tennis. I had found her hot button.

These buttons are not always easy to find. They vary greatly. Hobbies. Sports. Friends. Food. Weather. Tennis. Politics. Children. Macrame. Whatever.

Go right through the list. If you don't succeed at first, push another button. Eventually you'll find one marked "Hot." Make a mental note. If you want to keep the conversation moving, just push this button again. And again. And again.

4. LISTEN CARE-FULLY

Ninety percent of all communication is nonverbal. And any fool can tell whether the listener is truly involved or is just enduring the conversation. The speaker will usually hold back revealing inner secrets unless he or she knows that the listener truly cares about what is being said.

This is especially true with husbands and wives. Melissa Sands, founder of "Mistresses Anonymous" and author of the book, *The Making of the American Mistress,* reports that a mistress is much more than just an exciting sex partner who keeps her man bewitched. She is also an expert in the lost art of listening. A wise wife would do well to take note of the opposition's game plan.

Miss Sands writes, "Men have mistresses because they have needs that they are unable to fill in their other lives. By needs, I mean needs to communicate—sexually, verbally, tactfully."

Ironically, mistresses usually see their men at the *peak* of their day, both in energy and motivation. "So often," says Sands, "a married woman makes time for her job, her kids, the PTA, and her mother-in-law, but does not make a special time for her husband. A mistress does."

If your marriage is suffering from lack of communication, maybe it's time just to listen. Remember there is no perfect marriage; every couple experiences their low points. After all our years of a happy marriage, Charlie and I still have a hard time talking at times, especially when we have opposite opinions. But we try to be patient with each other and ride out any storm. So I would encourage you to hang in there until the fun returns.

Listen care-fully. Perhaps that's the essential ingredient in communication. If you really care, that care shines through. The word *wisdom* in Hebrew means, "A heart that listens." That's a heart with ears. Love listens. The two go hand in hand, or ear in ear.

12

LOVE

Sigmund Freud once asked, "What is it that women want?"

Why are we women such a mystery to men? Even though we are all unique, we have basically the same longings:

—We want to develop our talents and gifts.
—We want to feel satisfaction at the end of each day.
—We want to love and be loved.

Why is that such a mystery?

Throughout history, the single most popular theme of artists and authors alike is love. Love seems incapable of definition, yet it is that elusive elixir that men and women spend a lifetime chasing.

Pierre Teilhard de Chardin mused, "Someday, after we have mastered the winds, the waves, the tides, and gravity, we will harness for God the energies of love; and then, for the second time in the history of the world, man will have discovered fire."

The top-forty songs tell us that love is a flowery, sugary

feeling. But in reality, love is an act of the will. True love requires sacrifice and commitment. And, yes, sometimes, the joy and ecstasy follow.

Love takes many forms. As a mother, love is the heart-to-heart, late-night bedside chats with my girls. As a married woman, love is the tender embrace and intimate companionship with my husband. As a child of God, I am aware of another kind of love, without depth or measure.

According to Hollywood, "Love makes the world go 'round." Love is the theme of movies of all kinds whether they are rated R, PG, or G. In the ancient Greek language, the most precise language in the world, there are three words for love, each with a different meaning—erotic love, family love, and God's love.

1. R–Rated Love—For Adults Only

"Erotic love" is the meaning of the Greek word *eros*. Hollywood calls it R–Rated Love—For Adults Only. God designed erotic love for husbands and wives for their physical relationship in marriage. And marriage *is* for adults only.

Speaking of sex, the Pennsylvania Commerce Secretary once asked an aide to give him a list of all male and female employees in the department broken down by sex.

A few hours later, a memo from the aide was on his boss's desk which read, "We don't have any male or female employees broken down by sex, but we do have two alcoholics!"

Unfortunately, a few years after the honeymoon, many couples are broken down by sex. Phyllis Diller lamented that her marriage came to such a dead stop, she nicknamed their water bed, "Lake Placid."

So often I see the play "The Love Triangle" happening in real life. This long-running tragedy has been playing in local neighborhoods since the beginning of time, with slight variations.

Scene One: 4:25 P.M. Mrs. Burn-Out at the kitchen sink, tired and disheveled from dishes, diapers, and distractions. The baby's crying, the washer broke, and she just started her period.

Scene Two: 5:01 P.M. Mr. Uptight leaves an angry customer and demanding boss and heads for home, only to be cut off in traffic by a sports car with dark windows. He's mad, tired, and hungry when he pulls into his driveway.

Scene Three: 5:30 P.M. Mr. Uptight encounters Mrs. Burn-Out. Censored. Argument deemed too violent for family audience.

Scene Four: 9:48 P.M. Remarkable transformation takes place. Mr. Uptight turns into Herman Hot-to-Trot, while Mrs. Burn-Out becomes Nellie Not-Tonight. (Nellie wants her man to make up before she makes love, but he wants to make love in order to make up!)

Scene Five. 10:15 P.M. Mrs. Burn-Out is wiped out, heads for bed to sleep. Herman Hot-to-Trot heads for local bar to unwind.

Final Scene. 11:31 P.M. Enter the other woman. Love triangle complete.

Curtain Closes.

The Cave-Dweller Craver

A woman wrote last month from Louisiana to say, "My husband has had an affair with a woman for about a year. She is having the honeymoon I never had!"

Ladies, this is serious business. Your husband may be starving for love. Even if he seems cold and cynical, deep inside he has a need that only you can fill. Listen to *his* side of the story. Here is part of a letter I received from a man in Chicago.

"I would gladly live in a cave if I had someone I could really love and respect. I want to love my wife, if only she would warm up to me. I want to bring life and good into our marriage. I want the kids to be happy. I want them to be glad to bring their friends into our home. I am an animal that needs love. I'm a creation of almighty God and I want to feel like it. To love, and to be loved.

"Can you help me cope, so I don't break my promise to my kids about never leaving their mother again? I'm not a Francis of Assisi. Just a guy who craves love."

His is a true voice from the male side of the fence. I overheard another man tell his friend, "You can't believe the sex drive I have within me. It's like I have a 747 down inside of me. Unfortunately, my wife only has a Piper Cub inside of her! We don't match up very well."

Sex is to marriage what air conditioning is to an automobile. It can run without it, but it certainly is more fun with it.

Sex comforts a man, and soothes away his frustrations. Do you know what your husband is thinking about right now? He may be sitting in a meeting or driving to an appointment, but chances are he's hoping that tonight you'll soothe away his frustrations.

No matter how old he is, even if you think his flame has died, the coals are still smoldering (at least, I understand they are!). And you can rekindle that fire.

The Twenty-Four-Hour Affair

A man needs his wife to be his Number One cheerleader, whether he's down and out or supremely confident. His needs are still the same.

The wife of a Miami Dolphin football star told me, "My husband is so popular, no matter where we go he gets mobbed for autographs. The last thing he needs is another pat on the back from me."

I told her, "That's not so. He's looking for your praise more than all the others. Their cheers are hollow, but yours are special."

At a game the next week when her husband scored a touchdown, thousands stood and screamed for minutes. And then I watched him on the sideline as he turned and looked up into the crowd—not to watch the mob, but to look for his wife. He strained until he saw her and then grinned ear to ear and held the football up for her to see. Hers was the only face he saw.

Thoreau said, "Most men lead lives of quiet desperation." How sad. How unnecessary!

But ladies, it doesn't have to be that way. I believe that we wives can help spice up a tired marriage and rev up a run-down Fred. We can grab his attention, fill his heart with happiness, and keep his eyes focused on home.

Erotic love is not just a physical act late at night, but rather it's a twenty-four-hour affair. That means you have the joy of setting the scene for romance.

The Morning Farewell

Someone told me that the eight most important minutes of your husband's day are the first four minutes when he awakes and the first four minutes when he returns home. In other words, the mood for love (or the lack of it) is often set during either of these four-minute periods.

Around our house, the first four minutes involves the raising of the subconscious.

Charlie leaves very early for work. I know that if his last impression of me is a zombie in curlers, he may have second thoughts about coming home.

So I try to pull myself together as best I can. In spite of the early morning rush hour at our house (often with traffic backups at the bathrooms!), I walk with him to the front door and wave until he's out of sight. No big deal, but it has become a morning habit with me. My feet just head in that direction when Charlie announces, "I'm going."

A lady in Minnesota who tried this wrote, "I waved good-bye as my husband left for work. I even watched as he cleaned the frost off his window. He loved it. He almost plowed into a snowbank on the way up the driveway."

That's the idea! Life is a daring adventure or it's nothing. What a challenge to create sky-diving thrills within your own four walls.

The Office Call

I appeared at a charity function in Phoenix along with Erma Bombeck who was the Mistress of Ceremonies. "Inspire us, Marabel," she coaxed, "give us an assignment."

I told all those housewives, "Every husband needs excitement and high adventure at his own address."

"Now, ladies," I continued, "give your husband a little surprise. This afternoon, call him at work. When he answers, purr into the phone, 'Hi, Honey, I wanted you to know that I just crave your body. Hurry home. Bye!' "

Erma interrupted excitedly, "Wait a minute. I tried that! I called my husband at the office and when he answered, I said, 'Honey, I just crave your body.'

"And do you know what happened? He put me on hold!"

The sexy office phone call has received a lot of attention around the country. One time on "The Dinah Shore Show," a blonde actress interrupted me to ask, "Why not call him at the office and say, 'Hey big boy, hurry home. Here's what's waiting for you tonight: two all beef patties, special sauce, lettuce, cheese, pickles, onions, on a sesame seed bun!' "

Dinah interrupted her to ask, "Yes, but what if Fred comes home looking for a Big Mac and all he gets is an Egg McMuffin?"

McHousewife, go for it! Make your call right now. Your husband is hoping you will. Just don't plan a company dinner at 6:00 P.M. tonight!

The Welcome Home

I believe that a man can stand almost anything in marriage except boredom. In our first few years of marriage, I looked like a slob when Charlie came home at night. Sweating in grungy jeans, broom in hand, looking like The Totaled Woman, I wanted him to see how hard I worked. But to him, I looked the same at night as when he left home that morning. Unappealing!

Perhaps a woman can't finish her work and be cleaned up when Fred walks in the door every day. In fact, many women come home from work after Fred's already home, and if that's your case, give this book to Fred! But remember, your husband's most important sex organ is his *eye*. He may first need to get past the visual barrier of how you look before he can care how you feel.

In the book, *The Total Woman,* I told how I dressed up in a sexy outfit when Charlie came dragging home from work one evening. Charlie responded like gangbusters. Talk about electricity!

Creative women all across the country wanted to set the scene for excitement and high adventure in their houses. My mailbox is full of letters from you romantic women who cared enough to share your fun.

A woman from New Jersey wrote, "I didn't have any money to spend, so I had to find something around the house. I came up with a toy rifle, sombrero, and poncho and hid behind the door. When he came in, I told him to stick up his hands. Then I told him it was either his body or his life. He looked at me and just fell over across the table."

A wife in Maine wrote, "Wait till Dick sees my Christmas costume (hope it doesn't get too cold)—knee high black patent leather boots, two dazzling bows, and a six-foot scarf. I might stick some holly in my hair. He really goes for these crazy noncostumes, as we call them."

And a letter from California said, "Two weeks ago, while

rewinding a skein of yarn that my son had unwound, an idea struck me. After I put the kids to bed, I took the yarn and started at the front door and strung it all through the house with little inviting notes every few feet. I positioned myself in our candlelight bedroom in my nightie with the end of the yarn around my finger.

"My husband loved it," she wrote. "He said he couldn't believe I did it. So now when he comes home, we talk and hold hands a lot. Our love-making has become more romantic, and things seem to be running perfectly. We still have little misunderstandings, but at least we are talking. We are now able to forgive and forget.

"P.S.," she closed, "Tonight I cut footprints out of paper to lead him to our room. Each print has a sexy note on it. I never knew how exciting marriage could be. Thank you for the courage to try."

Your husband may be hoping that one night you'll meet him in an outrageously sexy outfit. If you do, he'll never forget it. And I guarantee he'll never again bring home anyone for dinner without calling first.

Dressing up in some sexy, outrageous outfit is guaranteed to produce results. You may not be able to predict what kind of results, but, like the cross-eyed javelin thrower, you'll at least get his attention!

One woman told me a classic story about a husband who had begun drinking to escape his nagging wife. The more she nagged, the more he drank. He came home later and later each evening.

His wife saw that her nagging was only making matters worse, so she formed a plan. One afternoon she prepared his favorite dinner, took a long, scented bubble bath, put on a sexy costume, and waited for his return home.

Meanwhile, Fred stopped off at the bar and proceeded to get smashed. Finally he arrived home in a stupor.

She met him at the door, took him in her arms, and kissed him. She removed his coat and escorted him to his favorite chair. Propping up his feet, she removed his shoes and turned on the TV. She brought him a hot cup of coffee and sat down on the arm of the chair.

She began to rub his shoulders and back. She kissed his neck and blew in his ear. Then she tugged at him and asked if he would care to go into the bedroom with her.

After pondering her proposal for a moment, he blurted out, "I might as well, I'm going to catch it when I get home anyway!"

Any jury would have acquitted this wife of murder! But fortunately for Fred, her attitude had changed. Now perhaps his would, too.

The Costume Party

On a Phil Donahue show, I once suggested a Halloween costume for wives. "After the trick or treaters have all gone to bed," I told the women, "take off all your clothes, slip into a pair of boots, trenchcoat, and a mask. Then sneak out the back door, come around, and ring the front doorbell. When your husband opens the door, throw open your coat and sing out, 'Trick or Treat!'"

Again, you creative women responded. After all the little goblins had gone, one lady put on a Frankenstein wig, boots, and trenchcoat and sneaked around to the front door. When her husband answered, she flashed her costume. He was stunned but recovered quickly. Then with obvious perception he grinned and said, "My, you're an old one, aren't you?"

But the top prize of perseverance goes to the lady from Indiana who wrote,

Dear Marabel,

You have improved my marriage 100 percent, but I must tell you about one flop I had.

My husband had been on a business trip for three weeks. By the time he got back, it was December and we had four inches of snow on the ground.

I waited for a few days after his return, then one night I put on a trenchcoat, boots, and floppy hat to shadow my face, and then crept out the back, went around to the front door and rang the bell.

My husband turned on the porch light and opened the door. I flung open my coat and said, "Trick or treat!"

He slammed and locked the door, then ran through the house yelling at me to come and look at the naked lady on the front porch. He didn't recognize me!

I rang the bell again and when he opened the door I opened my coat again.

He slammed and locked the door. He went through every room of the house calling me to hurry up and come see the lady on the step before she left. He still didn't know it was me!

Now by this time, I don't mind telling you, I was freezing. So I rang the bell and started yelling that *I* was the lady on the step.

He opened the door, I left my coat closed, then he

yelled at me, "What are you doing out there on the step like that?"

I was so cold I could care less about what he thought, so I yelled back, "I'm turning you on, can't you tell?"

My sweet husband was so embarrassed that he didn't recognize me, it took a couple of days for him to get over it. But it was well worth the try.

Thanks for the fun.

Love, Debbie

Marriage Repair Service

I received a letter from a lady who wrote, "My sister-in-law is having trouble experiencing an orgasm. Can you give me some tips that might help her?"

I was touched over her concern for her family!

What prevents women from having an orgasm? Why do some women not seem to enjoy sex as much as others? There have been scores of books written on the subject. I suggest you check one out of the library.

A poor sex relationship is often due to a lack of communication. He wants it but she doesn't, or vice versa. A lady from Dallas wrote, "Your book told my husband what I was unable to convey. In talking things out, he said he felt like I was making the nightly decisions about sex by what I wore to bed—black panties meant 'yes' and my old cotton meant 'I'm tired.' In essence he felt manipulated! What a discovery that was for me."

She explained how they worked out their problem. "I hung my nightgowns and pajamas in one section of my closet and put up a hook. Each night my husband puts on the hook what he wants me to wear. Sometimes I find an empty hook (and he *hasn't* forgotten!), and sometimes I find a new nightie. The decision is his and now he's happy! So am I!"

The number one killer of romance in marriage is fatigue. It takes energy to be a passionate lover. After chasing ankle-biters all day long, straightening the living room three times, plus doing four loads of wash, there's no way you can be a mad, passionate lover if you don't take your vitamins!

Get ready. Plan your day. Pace yourself so tonight you can send your husband into orbit. Jump off the dresser into his arms as he comes in from his shower. He won't forget that one for awhile. Make it a fun evening. He'll be flying past pigeons and satellites. Send him over the rainbow. You can do it. You, the red-hot, electric mama!

2. PG–RATED LOVE—PARENTAL GUIDANCE NECESSARY

Hello, Young Mothers

Hello, young mothers, wherever you are,
    I hope your downers are few.
All of my aspirin go with you tonight—
    I've been a mother like you.

Be brave, young mothers, and clean up the floor,
    Be quick, 'cause Fred's at the door.
Turn off the oven, the chicken's on fire.
    I've been a mother like you.

I know how it feels to have kids at your heels,
    And to carpool to school in a trance.
Your mother-in-law will be moving in soon,
    And you groan, not really by chance.

Don't give up, young mothers, whatever you do,
    Don't give up because you're run down.
All of my family are quiet tonight—
    They've been in bed since ten.

All of my family are quiet tonight.
    They've been in bed since ten!

The second Greek word for love is *philia*, meaning brotherly or family love.

Love is not something you *feel*, but what you *do*, especially in the family. When you're up at 2:00 A.M. with a sick child, you may not feel warm fuzzies, but you do it anyway. Love is an act of will.

Family love or parental love is an awesome responsibility. Family love implies that parental guidance is necessary.

Not long ago a teenage girl in Philadelphia who was planning to run away from home wrote to me. I believe she reflects the heart-cry of many teenagers today, and that's why I share her actual letter with you, but with a changed name.

Dear Mrs. Morgan:

I am writing to tell you that I understand runaways because I'm about to become one myself. I hope everything I tell you will show mothers the importance of accepting and understanding their kids . . . especially teenagers.

You know, I'm literally *terrified* of becoming a mother because I'm afraid I'll be the same to my daughter as my mother is to me. I'm afraid that in a moment of anger I'll spit out words that will scar my daughter for life. I remember a day a long time ago when my mother asked God what she did to deserve me, and I've resented her, even hated her, ever since.

I smoke pot because it makes me feel good. I suppose it's a substitute for the good feelings I lack from my family. When I'm out with my friends I drink my troubles away. If I get drunk I don't think about my parents. They don't exist as far as I'm concerned.

I used to tell them, "I love you." But I don't bother anymore. I have too much inside me to lie.

I have two older sisters and an older brother to compete with. Forget it. I gave up years ago. They won't be pleased until I fit their mold, so why be a hypocrite? I'm the black sheep of the family, so why disappoint them? But deep in the back of my mind I *wish* they would have been my friends.

Enclosed is my runaway letter to my parents. Thank you.

Jan Bart

(My name is Barton, but I can't bring myself to write it. So, my friends call me Bart.)

I wanted to write her back, but when I looked at the envelope, there was no return address or phone number. My heart sank. (By the way, Jan—and you will know your real name—if you happen to read this book, please write back. I would love to talk with you.)

I then opened a copy of Jan's good-bye letter to her folks. I know that she would want me to share this with you for the help it might bring.

Dear Mom and Dad:

How do you write a letter when you know you're gonna be leaving?

My one wish in life was to be loved. That's all. That's it. All I ever wanted or could ask for was to be loved. Loving requires understanding, not demands. I can't be what you want me to be. I know you're disappointed with me, but so am I.

Do you know the dictionary meaning of the word "disappoint"? "To *fail* to satisfy the hopes and expectations of . . ."

How would you like to live with that? How would you like to know that you're a total failure?

I never really seem to please you.

You never loved me for what I am, but for what *you wanted* me to be.

You say my friends are rotten, my music is bad, my clothes aren't good enough for you.

So . . . I thought about it a lot. I am leaving tonight and getting out of your hair. I know you'll have the whole police force out after me, and when and if they find me, I'll be returned to my home and sentenced to spend my days on the truck, and my nights in the sewing room. I'm scared only for that.

Don't worry about me, because if I'm as bad as you say I am, I shouldn't be allowed to live anyway. I figure I'll be no great loss.

Sometimes I think I'll regret it later, but then I see Dad coming after me because "I slammed the car door." I look at my arm, I see bruises, but I can't see love.

I can see the future now. I can envision the whole thing. A year from now I'll come walking up the front sidewalk, ring the doorbell, someone will answer it, spit in my face and tell me never to come back again.

So what do I do? Should I stay and be told how rotten I am? Should I apologize for being so wicked and evil like you think I am? Or should I just leave and forget everything? I'm just a "stupid little brat." I'm leaving.

Well, to conclude, I wish we could have been friends. Maybe we will someday with a little more understanding. That's it right there, it's all wrapped up in that one word—understanding.

Thank you for everything you ever gave me. I appreciate it. I had more possessions than three kids my age and I won't forget it.

Take it easy, and I'll see you again someday. Hopefully, we'll all be much kinder.

Good-bye.

Love,
Jan

P.S. I simply couldn't be what everyone *else* wants. I've got to be me.

* * *

Why do so many children grow up thinking they are *not* loved? Many parents feel that by providing a home, meals, and clothes they have expressed their love. Yet their children don't perceive that as love.

Rearing children is perhaps the most demanding of all professions. PG–13 was adopted by the movie industry to help warn parents about movies too violent or suggestive for children under thirteen. That Pre-Thirteen Era is the most impressionable period in a child's life. Parental guidance *is* necessary—day after day after day.

I believe that a mother expresses her love to her children in two main ways—through warning and warming.

Warning

I spoke to a group of teenage girls recently on three assigned topics—good grooming, make-up, and sex. I had forgotten how intimidating ninth-grade girls, with purple eyeshadow, scarlet pouty lips, and unabashed, youthful beauty, can be.

To establish rapport, I first talked about hair styles for different shaped faces and a few diet tricks, and then I switched gears to guys.

"As I tell my own girls," I told them, "you can't wait until you're pressed up against a warm body in the back seat with the moon over Miami to decide what your moral standards are going to be."

After class was over, an exquisite, voluptuous fourteen-year-old hurried up to talk to me. "How did you know?" she whispered, her young face strained with worry.

I must have looked puzzled. "What you said," she continued, "about being pressed, you know . . . with the moon over Miami? That was me—last night!"

I believe that lots of ninth-graders face a similar situation every night. One girl told her mother, "Things are different now, Mom. It isn't like when you were young. We don't have to worry about pregnancy, so what's the big deal? As long as you really *care* about someone, why not make love? I don't see anything wrong with it."

Why should she? For a decade or more the media and the movies have given our young people a steady dose of "sexual freedom." Mere children feel the pressure to jump into bed on the first date. Some don't even know they have another option.

If you have pre-adolescent children, now is the time to prepare them for the onslaught of sexual overtures they are certain to encounter as teenagers. Sex education starts early.

The Friday Night Party

The worst thing about being a parent of teenagers is that you're traveling on unchartered ground. No matter how many guidebooks you read or parent-effectiveness courses you take, the variable is that energetic, lethargic, precious, obstinate teenager.

My friend, whose daughter was three years older than Laura, kept telling me, "Just you wait. It's awful!"

Sure enough, right on schedule at 3:00 P.M. on the first day of school in the ninth grade, Laura changed into a typical teenager.

She left for school that morning a sweet, co-operative, darling daughter. She returned home at 3:30 that afternoon a sneering, sullen, surly teenager.

No "Hi, Mom." No kisses. Just growls and sneers. If I asked any questions, she only curled her lip at me.

When her girlfriends came over, it was a gathering of the Sneers, the Leers, and the Curled Lips. All of her friends were surly. The whole school seemed surly.

3:30 P.M.

I couldn't believe my eyes. Her personality had totally changed in the span of eight hours!

Our relationship deteriorated rapidly. I didn't know what to expect or how to react. I tried to be upbeat, but it didn't make any difference.

The confrontations were daily. Hourly. One afternoon we had a big argument about a party she wanted to attend that night. Upperclassmen and college kids were throwing the party, and had invited Laura and a few of her friends. I told her she couldn't go, but I couldn't give concrete reasons why.

Laura stood towering over me, defiant, her eyes flashing with anger. "I can walk right out that door and go to that party and you can't stop me," she shouted.

"I know you can walk out of here, Laura, if you want to, but I don't believe you will. You're a Morgan, and Morgans handle their problems differently." (I didn't know if Morgans do or not, but I held my breath.)

She was thinking it over. With new courage I went on, "I do understand how you feel, Honey. I wish you could go. I wish you could do everything you want to do—but there may be problems in this situation."

"What problems?" she suddenly shot back.

"I can't even say, Laura. I don't know specifically. But I'm responsible to God for you, and I feel so strongly that you shouldn't go. You have to trust me."

215

Although my heart was pounding, I tried to act cool. She glared at me with hatred—my firstborn, this fourteen-year-old child/woman—and then stomped into her bedroom and slammed the door.

She didn't go to the party that night, but the tension in our house was unbearable. In fact, we had unbearable tension for a year and a half. Charlie and I began to feel like we were losing our daughter.

I cried out to God, "Lord, help me. Help us!" I stared often at the sign on my desk, "IT'S ALWAYS TOO SOON TO GIVE UP." And I didn't.

I told Laura, "I love you. We have given our lives to raise you right, and I'm not going to let *anybody* undo what we have done. I'm going to *fight* for you."

She knew I meant it. She knew I loved her. We could both recall our years of fun times together:

—All the walks, window-shopping, and licking ice-cream cones.

—All my listening to her silly, inane conversations.

—All the canceling of my plans to be at her football, volleyball, and softball games.

But it paid off. The love held. Those years of togetherness and sacrifice held. We made it through the storm.

Pressure City

I remember when Laura was a junior in high school. One day she informed me, "Mom, everything I hear and see out in the world, at school, with my friends, wherever I go—everything runs counter to what you tell me is true."

Do you sometimes feel like a voice crying in the wilderness? I do. But I know that if I'm the only voice giving truth to my teenagers, I dare not stop!

One lazy summer afternoon as Laura and I slathered suntan lotion over each other's backs, she began to talk about a young stewardess she had met at the pool.

"She told me about her friends who had had abortions," Laura said. "Then she asked me, 'Who's *your* gynecologist?'

"I said, 'I don't have one.'

"She couldn't believe it. She said, 'You don't have a gynecologist?' "

As Laura and I talked about the loose morals of today, I told her, "Women tell me all the time, 'If only I could do it over.' "

One friend said, "We had to get married, and it has put an unbelievable strain on our marriage over the years. And the worst time was last week when my daughter found out about it! If only I could do it over."

As mothers, we face downers each day. So do our teenagers. And I must say, theirs are probably more monumental. Maybe your washer broke down today, but your daughter may lose her virginity tonight!

Their pressures come from their peers—pressures to perform and conform. Pierre Pressure comes in many disguises, and though his line may be different, the consequences are the same—the guilt, the depression, and the loneliness. No wonder teenagers in desperation often turn to alcohol and drugs for relief.

The Stoned Age

Midway through the tenth grade, Laura's high school Fellowship of Christian Athletes chapter began meeting at our house on Monday nights. The meeting was opened to all student athletes. "Wall-to-wall puberty," Charlie called it.

The first night I noticed that some of the kids could hardly make it through the door. Their eyes were glazed as they stumbled to a sofa and sat in a daze through the meeting.

"Charlie, those kids are stoned!" I whispered frantically behind the closed kitchen door. "What are we going to do?"

"We'll love them," he answered gently. "Maybe they'll find answers here, and they won't need drugs anymore."

We did love them and tried to "be there" for those teenagers. But I couldn't understand why they would risk so much, when they had so much going for them. These were not the *bad* kids, these were the star athletes and beauty queens. Why the need for drugs?

I asked Jim Hoag, director of the Renaissance Center, a drug rehabilitation center in Miami. He had become hooked on drugs at the age of fourteen.

Hoag told me, "The first time I took cocaine, I thought, *Wow, this is the most wonderful thing that's ever happened to me!* I was in love with it, more than anything in the world. I didn't grow slowly into drug dependence. It was an instant addiction with an insatiable appetite."

As he spoke, he became increasingly animated. "With the drug, I could do anything. I was willing to risk anything to get it."

He repeated intensely, "*Anything!* I had to have it. The consequences were irrelevant because I *loved* it."

My astonishment must have shown on my face. "Listen," he said, "the love affair with the drug exceeds the love you have for your wife, your friend, or your parents. Having cocaine is like being married. It is as enticing as a lover. And just like marriage, it requires commitment and loyalty. I wanted to talk about it with my friends. I looked forward to being with it. It was a marriage between me and the substance. But a fourteen-year-old is too immature to be married."

Hoag continued, "I didn't start out as a 'bad kid.' My dad was vice president of Magnavox. I had everything I wanted, but it wasn't enough. Dad was so busy that we didn't spend much time together. I had little accountability to anyone."

Hoag advises parents, "All the preliminary work with the child has to be done before the child reaches the age of twelve. After that, the kid doesn't hear a word the parent says because peer pressure is stronger than parent pressure."

The "preliminary work" is prevention therapy, and prevention therapy sure beats rehabilitation therapy—both for the child *and* the parents.

Warming

The preliminary work is what I call *warming*. Children need not only warning but also warming.

One semester Michelle was required to perform an experiment with plants for her science project. We stopped at the garden shop and she picked up two geranium plants. At home she headed for the backyard and placed one on either side of the yard.

"I am trying to determine what happens if you are kind to a plant," she explained. "So, I'm going to be sweet to one of the plants the entire semester, and be mean to the other one."

Every morning and afternoon she hurried outside to speak to the plants. On one side of the yard she cooed, "Oh, look at my sweet baby. How beautiful you look today! You are the dearest little plant in the world. You are doing so well. Your leaves are just lovely. I'm so proud of you. Keep it up. I'll be back soon!"

Then she trotted over to the other plant and gave it a loud thrashing, "You despicable plant. You are so ugly. You haven't grown an inch since yesterday. You haven't bloomed. You haven't done anything. Oh! I can hardly bear to look at you. Disgusting! What are you good for, anyway? Just an ugly shriveled-up plant!"

I laughed when Michelle went out each day to praise and scream, and I hoped that the neighbors weren't watching. At the end of two months, she prepared a comparison chart showing only slight differences in the two plants.

But the surprise came the day before she was to turn in the report. Michelle came running into the house, "Mom, Mom, come look at this! The ugly plant has grown horns!"

I looked and, sure enough, the "despicable" plant had grown horns. Not thorns, but horns, almost like the tongue of a snake. A forked horn was coming out of each flower!

Now, I am not sure what significance that might have. Scientifically I can't say whether yelling at a plant will produce horns, but I do know that constant screaming at a child will produce insecurity, hostility, and resentment.

I also know that kind, loving words given daily to a tender child can produce wonders. A word of encouragement each day is the best fertilizer for self-esteem and a vital element in PG love.

Smellable Huggables

The other morning I found Michelle blow-drying her hair in the bathroom. I hugged her and said, "I *missed* you last night, Honey."

She looked surprised and said, "I was just in the next room."

"I know," I said, "but I still missed you."

She grinned. She was extremely cooperative all day!

Children form their self-esteem (or lack of it) by how their parents relate to them. As soon as kids toddle out into the world, their playmates begin chipping away at their self-image by putting them down and often making fun of them. Kids can be unbelievably cruel.

But that's where the mother comes in. In the evening she gathers the troops together and tends to the wounded. "Who's hurting tonight?" Then the mother, the self-esteem restorer, flies into action with her encouragement kit.

One of the best ways to encourage is also the easiest. Hug and kiss your kids every day, no matter what their age. Ruffle their hair, sock them in the arm, roughhouse with them. Some kind of reassuring physical contact is essential. Psychiatrists say that this, perhaps more than any other factor, may help keep your kids out of the psychiatrist's office later in life.

Now it's an easy thing for young mothers to hug and kiss

their little ones because they are so huggable and kissable. When my girls were babies, I could hardly put them down. But as soon as babies grow into little ankle-biters, they become smellier and nastier, and if you try to kiss them, they may kick you in the shins.

Do it anyway. And when they turn into teenagers and they snarl and spit in your eye, keep on hugging, even if they don't respond.

Granted, it's hard to hug a stiff kid, but it's so important. I believe that a lot of teenagers sleep around—just to feel *someone's* arms around them.

Remember when photographer Chris Wilder kidnapped and murdered a dozen or so beautiful young women as he crossed the country? He became the Number One Most Wanted Criminal on the FBI list.

During that time, a caller on a Miami talk show asked WIOD hostess Sandy Peyton, "How could these young women be so easily lured away by his dumb line, 'You are beautiful! Let me photograph you and make you a star'?"

Sophisticated Sandy Peyton surprised me with her answer. With sadness in her voice, she answered, "In this cold cruel world, we are all so lonely and looking for a kind word, I guess we're willing to do anything to get it."

Mothers, do you hear it? Whoever gives the warming gains the allegiance of the child.

So today, instead of criticizing your kids, compliment them. Find something to praise. You'll be glad you did, and so will they.

Raisin' Brains

A parent's love not only helps build a child's self-esteem

and keep him out of the psychiatrist's office, it may also make him smarter!

That's right. Warming can actually raise his IQ. Can you believe it?

For many years, the Berkeley Growth Studies analyzed children psychologically and intellectually and discovered, "a boy's IQ can be damaged by maternal neglect or abuse—IQs of boys could be correlated with hostile or loving mothering. *The loving mothers produced brighter sons.*"

Dr. Raymond Moody, author of the bestseller, *Life After Life,* reports a similar study. In an ordinary classroom filled with ordinary students, the teacher was told, "These six children have genius level IQs," although actually the six had been selected arbitrarily.

At the end of the year, all of the students were tested again. The six "genius" students rose appreciably in their IQ test scores, while the other children remained the same.

Why? The extra care and attention shown the special six, whether consciously or unconsciously, resulted in raising their IQs. The children rose to the level of expectation.

What a tremendous privilege lies in the hands of parents, grandparents, teachers, and anyone working with children— the privilege of molding a life.

President James Garfield once passed a young newsboy standing on the street corner. The President bowed to the boy as he passed by. His aide was surprised and asked him, "Mr. President, I noticed that you bowed to that boy. Did you know him?"

"No," the President replied, "but I bowed because no one knows *who* is buttoned up in the coat of that little boy."

Who knows who is buttoned up in the coat of *your* little one? No one knows, yet. Your love may make the difference.

3. G–RATED LOVE—GOOD NEWS FOR ALL AGES

The third word for love in the Greek is *agape*—God's love, unconditional and unending.

Sometimes a woman puts an unrealistic burden on her husband by expecting him to meet her deepest longings. He can't do it. No man on earth can fully meet a woman's needs; neither can any woman completely fulfill a man. God made us so that only *He* can meet the heart's deepest needs.

Whether our family or friends love us is not the ultimate issue. Sometimes they will and sometimes they won't. But we can be assured that God will love us, always. That news is worth passing on.

The phone rang one day and my friend's voice sounded breathless and urgent. "I didn't know if you'd heard. Martha is dying of cancer. Her son is getting married at Christmas, but the doctor just told her she may not live to see the wedding. I feel we ought to go see her as soon as possible."

I was leaving on a trip the next morning, so the only time I had was now. "Let's go now, Nancy. Give me ten minutes to get ready, and I'll bring some brownies from the freezer."

We arrived at Martha's front door, resolved to share God's life-giving message.

Martha, though obviously in pain, was gracious and chatted happily about the upcoming wedding. Our time was short so I eased right in, "Martha, you know that God loves you. Perhaps you remember the verse, 'For God loved the world so much (that's you) that he gave his only Son (that's Jesus) so that anyone who believes in him (that can be you) shall not perish but have eternal life.'

"Do you believe that, Martha?" I asked.

"Oh, yes," she said. "I pray to Him every day."

"Would you like to ask Him into your life as your own Savior?"

"Yes, I would," she answered firmly.

She started to move off the sofa to kneel down, but grimaced in pain.

"That's all right," I told her. "You don't have to kneel. Just sit here and invite Him in."

Martha prayed the words softly, then added, "And please help me to be a good servant of Yours."

When I looked up, her face shone with joy. God had given her His peace. And with Him as her Savior, she was prepared for whatever the future held.

The Exchanged Life

Tim Hansel, in his book *When I Relax I Feel Guilty,* wrote: "When God chose to reveal Himself uniquely, He did it through a person, through a life-style—because He knew then, as now, that what we are is far more potent than what we say. Two thousand years ago God declared unambiguously in the life of Jesus Christ that human flesh is a good conductor of divine electricity—and, as far as I understand, He hasn't changed His mind."

The living God offered me a deal that I personally couldn't refuse—it's called The Exchanged Life. I brought to Him my failures, my "garbage," the whole mess, and I dumped it at His feet.

In exchange (and those are the key words), He gave me Himself and His life-changing qualities of love, peace, joy, and power, all of which He has unlimited supply. Jesus is not dead. He's alive! That dead Man got up and walked, and He's here right now as you read these words.

You may not be convinced that such an incredible offer could be true, but perhaps you may be inclined to test Him.

Excellent! Whenever you tentatively reach out to God, however you say it is acceptable. I suggest something like this: "God, help me. Somehow show me you are real. I would love to make the Great Exchange, giving you all my heartache and failure, and receiving from you forgiveness and abundant life."

What a message of hope. And when that ultimate downer comes, which is death, God will turn even that into an upper!

Orphans Welcome

Harlan Howard wrote a song* about a little boy who came into the kitchen one evening while his mother was cooking dinner. He handed her a paper on which he had written:

Bill	
For mowing the yard	$ 5.00
Making my own bed this week	1.00
Going to the store	.50
Playing with little brother while you went to the store	.25
Taking out the trash	1.00
Getting a good report card	5.00
Raking the yard	2.00
Total owed	$14.75

*© 1974 by Tree Publishing Co., Inc. and Harlan Howard Songs International Copyright Secured. All Rights Reserved. Used by permission.

His mother looked at him standing there expectantly, and a thousand memories flashed through her mind. So she picked up the pen, turned the paper over, and wrote:

For the nine months I carried you growing inside me,	No Charge
For the nights I've sat up with you, doctored you, prayed for you,	No Charge
For the time and the tears that you cost through the years,	There's No Charge
When you add it all up, the full cost of my love is	No Charge
For the nights filled with dread and the worries ahead,	No Charge
For the advice and knowledge and the cost of your college,	No Charge
For the toys, food and clothes and for wiping your nose,	There's No Charge
When you add it all up, the full cost of my love is	No Charge

When the little boy finished reading, he looked up at his mother with tears in his eyes, and said, "Mom, I sure do love you." Then he took the pen and in great big letters he wrote, "Paid in full."

What this mother did for her son is exactly what God has done for us. Our debt for sin was "paid in full." And the full cost of God's love is "no charge."

At the end of the movie *Annie,* the sky lights up with a fantastic display of Fourth of July fireworks. Little Orphan Annie snuggles up to Daddy Warbucks and with her face glowing with joy, whispers, "Now I finally have a daddy."

If you're an orphan today, your heavenly Father is waiting with outstretched arms. He wants to light up your life like the Fourth of July.

LOOKING AHEAD

One Saturday afternoon, Michelle and I were cleaning out her closet when we found a jewelry box behind some books. She lifted out a necklace and said, "Oh Mom, look how beautiful this is. Did they wear necklaces like this when you were alive?"

I was shocked. "Michelle," I shouted, "I *am* alive!"

I can remember when I was Michelle's age thinking my own mother was old (thirty was middle age, forty was ancient). But *my* child thought I was dead!

Talk about a wipeout! I would have laughed, but I was too tired after spending a day that was a cross between a circus and a zoo. Actually, I wasn't too sure myself that I had come through it alive.

But this morning I feel great. Hopefully, I've got a few more miles left on this body I call home.

Have you stopped to think that in only a short time it will be 1999, and then the end of the century, the year 2000. Sounds like science-fiction stuff, doesn't it?

Last spring I attended a two-week congress of several dozen leaders from various fields. We were gathered together to speculate about where we would be at the turn of the century. (I was there because they wanted a view from the kitchen sink!)

One of the speakers from Cornell University pointed out that in 1938, President Roosevelt had convened a similar group to advise him on what might happen in the next decade. The delegates tried to anticipate upcoming inventions and trends. They listed every invention conceivable. But in spite of their efforts, they failed to predict penicillin and radar and television and rockets and the atomic bomb, all of which were developed within the next five years.

What a world we live in! What an incredible time to be alive.

President Reagan, in his first public speech following the assassination attempt on his life by John Hinckley, addressed the Notre Dame graduation ceremonies. Looking ahead into the twenty-first century, he told of a recent study made by the Hudson Institute.

In the year 2010, life expectancy should have risen from 73 to 92. The work week will be cut in half. Man will be three times as productive, leaving more free time for leisure and recreation. Our energy problems will be over because of new energy sources. Medicine will have developed many body replacement parts. Space technology will be commonplace. Star-Wars type spaceships will shuttle travelers like buses.

"But most significantly," President Reagan pointed out, "is that ninety percent of the appliances, tools, games, and other items we will be using have not yet been invented."

High-Tech Mother

Try to imagine just what those yet uninvented items will be. Think of it.

What will a twenty-first century salesperson be selling? What aircraft will we be flying? What new math will your grandchildren be learning? What will you be cooking? Or wearing? Or driving? Or watching?

Who will be inventing those yet uninvented creations? Who will develop the undeveloped?

Could you? Will you?

And if not you, what kind of woman will she be?

Wonder Woman? A housewife? A secretary? A salesperson? Your own daughter?

You home executives, you working women, and you teenagers, you can shape tomorrow. All it takes is a vision that sees beyond the visible. Don't be afraid to risk. Remember, when the creative person leads, others will follow. Every creative person first had a dream. Every inventor first thought of a new and different way.

Peanut Power

Reflecting back on his career, the great black scientist, George Washington Carver, was asked what first sparked his interest as a scientist. His friend Glenn Clark recorded his reply in his biography *The Man Who Talks with the Flowers.*

Dr. Carver went into his laboratory one day and said, "Dear Mr. Creator, please tell me what the Universe was made for."

The Great Creator answered, "You want to know too much for that little mind of yours. Ask for something more your size."

Then Carver asked, "Dear Mr. Creator, what was man made for?"

Again the Great Creator replied, "Little man, you still are asking too much. Cut down the extent of your request and improve the intent."

So Carver asked, "Please Mr. Creator, will you tell me about the peanut?"

And the Creator replied, "That's better, but even that's infinite."

And He taught Carver how to take the peanut apart and put it together again, and again, and again. Eventually he discovered over 350 new uses for the peanut, including plastics and paint. His discoveries revolutionized the face of agriculture in the South.

Dr. Carver's advice to aspiring students still holds true today, "Start where you are with what you have. Make something of it, and never be satisfied."

Thank you, Dr. Carver.

What is your peanut? What's ahead for you? It may not be a computer robot or a laser beam or a cure for cancer, but rather something the size of a peanut.

Never underestimate little things. We all know what grand oak trees little acorns turn out to be.

So what about that little nut of yours? The one you are watering and nurturing each day?

Some day . . . it may flourish, and who knows how many it in turn may influence? As Helen Kromer wrote in the musical play *For Heaven's Sake:*

One man awake can awaken another.
The second can waken his next-door brother.
The third awake can raise the town by
    turning the whole place upside down.
And the many awake can make such a fuss,
    they finally awaken the rest of us,
One man up with the sun in his eyes . . . multiplies.*

The Unsung Symphony

Indian poet Rabindranath Tagore wrote, "I have spent my life stringing and unstringing my instrument, and the song I came to sing remains unsung."

What an indictment. What a horrible self epitaph. Even before he passes on.

Supreme Court Justice Oliver Wendell Holmes decried the nonuse of talent, "Alas, for those who never sing, but die with all their music in them."

Has the world heard your song? Have you started to sing? A friend told me recently, "If I could live my life over, I would do so many things differently."

Well, you'll never have that opportunity. So, start today and explore your possibilities, here and now. Four final tips.

1. *Start Small.* Think peanuts and acorns and atoms and babies.

* *For Heaven's Sake* copyright by Helen Kromer, 1961. Reprinted by permission of Baker's Plays, Boston, MA 02111.

2. *Enlarge Your Vision.* Alfred Nobel was a self-made businessman who invented dynamite and then built the first multi-national company to sell it. His Nobel Prize for Peace is bestowed annually upon those who during the preceding year have conferred the greatest benefit on mankind.

John Stevens, managing editor of *Leaders* magazine, notes that the Nobel Prize "is the one prize you can win without three doctoral degrees, an electron microscope, or even a remote comprehension of spelling or cash flow.

"Time is of the essence," he writes. "Prizes are not awarded posthumously. Besides, the world needs peace now."

The world needs *you* . . . now.

3. *Overcome Barriers.* Famed British journalist Malcolm Muggeridge was once asked about Soviet dissident Alexander Solzhenitsyn, whose gifted voice could not be stilled by the Iron Curtain, "What if oppression came to the rest of the world? Could Solzhenitsyn then be silenced?"

"If the whole world were encased in concrete," Muggeridge replied, "somewhere there would be a crack, and out of that crack there would come a flower, out of which would come the voice of Solzhenitsyn."

May you also be remembered as a concrete-cracking flower.

4. *Finish Strong.* The motto of my friend, Jim Bouderis, is what drives him onward each day—"Upon the threshold of victory lies the countless bones of thousands, who hesitated, withered and died."

With the various tools mentioned on the pages of this book, you can cross over the threshold to victory defusing negative electrical charges and converting them into positive opportunities.

Energy and warmth and light can flow through you to a

depressed, cold, and dark world. You can be the person you have always wanted to be and energize others with your electricity.

Scripture says, "As a man thinks in his heart, so is he." You can *choose* to be enthusiastic, to look for the good in the bad, knowing that even downers are part of the plan for your life.

Now you can live your days to the fullest, expecting favor from both God and man. People will be drawn to your radiance. The air will fairly crackle around you. You—the electric woman. Dynamic. Life giving.

Remember, it's not so important how you started out in this life, it's how you finish that counts.

"It's not how high you jump," evangelist D. L. Moody once said, "but how you walk after you land." It's not how deep your downer, but how you turn it into victory.

Go for the Gold

Do you remember the 1980 Winter Olympic Games at Lake Placid? What American can forget that memorable hockey game between the United States and Russia?

No one had expected the U.S. team to advance to the semi-finals. Other countries had sent their professional hockey teams, but our boys were only college amateurs.

Yet, night after night, Americans watched on TV as the U.S. came from behind to win over Czechoslovakia, Norway, East Germany, eight teams in all. Finally, they faced the Soviets, the Russian team that had toured America the month before and beaten its all-pro teams.

That night, against all odds, the young U.S. team played their hearts out and won the game! Then, after beating Finland, they won the gold medal as well. A tremendous cheer went up all over America. It just may have been the greatest victory of the century.

But do you know what happened in the locker room *before* the game? Congressman Jack Kemp told our family the rest of the story.

Coach Herb Brooks wondered what to tell his team. He knew they were scared to death. But here it is. Time for the pre-game pep talk. The final meeting. What do you tell a team of teenagers facing the greatest professional hockey team in the world?

He didn't give them a pep talk, as they sat in the locker room—silent and nervous and scared. But just as they were ready to skate out onto the ice, Coach Brooks looked at his boys and said, "Gentlemen, you were born to be athletes. This is your moment. Let's go."

Ladies, you were born to be electric. This is *your* moment. Let's go!

To contact Marabel Morgan, write:

Marabel Morgan
P.O. Box 380277
Miami, FL 33138